Hazel Was a Good Girl
Solving the Murder That Inspired Twin Peaks

Jerry C. Drake

CLASH
NON-FICTION

Hazel Was a Good Girl Press

"*Hazel Was A Good Girl* is a haunting and exhilarating journey into the heart of darkness of a time and place that will shake you to your core."

— S.A. Cosby, author of *All the Sinners Bleed*

"*Hazel Was a Good Girl* explores how the time period's class system and victim blaming led to the case of Hazel Drew being unsolved for over a century. Drake lays out a feasible conclusion to the identity of the perpetrator(s) of this crime. A great read."

— Betty Frizzell, author of *If You Can't Quit Cryin', You Can't Come Here No More* and former Chief of Police, Winfield, MO

"This meticulously researched book kicks away the shiny veneer of Gilded Age glitz and the dreamlike fantasy of *Twin Peaks* to reveal the haunting story of who killed the woman who inspired Laura Palmer. With a sharp eye for evidence and a methodical approach to investigation, Drake peels back the layers of lies and legend, shedding light on the perils that shadowed Hazel's quest for a life beyond her working-class roots. *Hazel Was a Good Girl* is a riveting exploration of class, corruption, ambition, and the relentless quest for truth that transcends time."

— Eddie McNamara, author of *Zodiactually: The Real Story of a Fake Serial Killer* (March 2026)

NON-FICTION

Hazel Was A Good Girl
Copyright © 2025 by Jerry C. Drake
Cover by Matthew Revert
ISBN: 9781960988591 (paperback)

CLASH Books
Troy, NY
clashbooks.com
Distributed by Consortium
All rights reserved.

First Edition: 2025

For Hazel Drew

Concordia Salus

CONTENTS

Hazel Was a
Good Girl

PART ONE
HAZEL WAS A GOOD GIRL

THE GIRL IN THE WATER

CHAPTER 1

I don't believe in ghosts, but I've seen a ghost and her name is Hazel Drew.

In the sweltering summer of 1908, during a late-night rendezvous in a remote wooded spot near the industrial city of Troy, New York, someone killed Hazel Irene Drew, tossing her body into a farmer's mill pond, where it was found a few days later. Hazel's death was a national story of interest for the month of July 1908, with newspapers as far away as the Kaiser's Germany filling their front pages with rumors of jilted jealous lovers, prostitution, pregnancy, and scandal.

Then, nothing.

By the end of July, the whole thing was over. The local authorities failed to name a killer and Hazel faded into obscurity until about eighty years later, when the tragedy of her death inspired the creation of a cult television series. David Lynch's *Twin Peaks* (1990-1991) was co-written by Mark Frost, whose grandmother lived near where Hazel was murdered and where, according to her, Hazel's ghost still haunted the Upstate New York woods.

The parallels between Hazel Drew and the fictional character she inspired, Laura Palmer, are clear. Unlike Laura Palmer, there was no Agent Dale Cooper on the scene to unravel Hazel Drew's death and to this day that murder remains unsolved.

The investigators at the time never developed any serious suspects (at least publicly) and interest in Hazel, despite the compelling mystery surrounding her death, has never taken hold in the "true crime community." There are podcast episodes here and there, and two other books have been written about her. We mainly know about Hazel today because of her connection to *Twin Peaks.*

Though I was a fan of the show growing up, I never had any idea it was inspired by real events. In a bizarre plot twist, I was drawn to the tale in much the same manner as Agent Cooper: through a dream. When I sat down to write this book it took me about a year to put that sentence on paper because it's never been my intention in life to be anything other than a hard-nosed skeptic.

To admit that Hazel Irene Drew came into my life in *a fucking dream* took some courage. Maybe I got obsessed, maybe I went a little crazy. Then again, maybe ghosts are real, and Hazel Drew is still out there trying to get her story told. You decide.

Let's rewind to the final months of 2019, before COVID drove the whole damn world mad. My friend announced to me that she and her husband were buying a house and planning to move themselves and their publishing business to the town of Troy, New York, an old Upstate industrial city on the Hudson. I was excited for this — it brought them closer. Also, I like the Albany region and was looking forward to having an excuse to spend more time exploring there.

We planned to meet up after my birthday once they had settled in the new place so that I could help with some crafty projects. Then came the dreams. My friend dreamed that a strange woman appeared in a room of her future house and offered her a book. It was turquoise in color, the title read: *The Absence of Memory.* She told me of this dream and we puzzled over its significance but found nothing that made sense in dream symbolism terminology.

A few days later as I was sick in bed, shivering with fever in my DC condo, I fell into a heavy sleep and encountered this book myself. In my dream I opened the book, a hardback, and saw that the first blank page contained a bookplate that read: *Ex Libris* Hazel I. Drew. *Ex Libris* is Latin for "from the library of" and was a common moniker on bookplates a century ago.

I slept for a few more hours and woke sweating from sickness. I took a shower and made some tea. Still intrigued by the dream I searched for "Hazel I. Drew" online. The first article to come up was from Find A Grave. I read Hazel's entry, which laid out in a few paragraphs what I have come to call the Legend of her life and death:

> More than a century ago, the body of 20-year-old Hazel Drew was found floating in Teal's Pond near the bottom of Taborton Mountain in Sand Lake, New York. An autopsy found that she'd died of blunt head trauma to the back of her head prior to ending up in the pond. Her death was labeled a murder...
>
> ...In the end, all the leads the investigators had run out. Nobody was ever arrested or charged with the murder, and to this day - Hazel Drew's murder remains unsolved!
>
> Hazel Drew was one of several children of John and Julia A. (Taylor) Drew. Her known siblings were Joseph, who was 2 years older than her, Carrie, who was 7 years younger, William who was 10 years younger, Emma who was 11 years younger, Emery who was 12 years younger but predeceased her, and Thomas who was 13 years younger, who also predeceased her.
> [1]

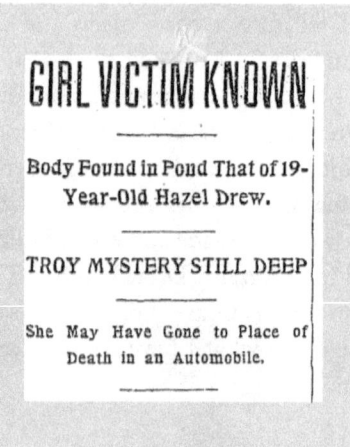

Washington Post, July 14, 1908. The case was already being covered in the Washington Post by the time Hazel Drew's body was identified. It became a major national news story in the summer of 1908.

On my initial reading the only thing that really jumped out at me was the fact that Hazel's murder had taken place in New York State, where my friend was moving. I had never heard of Sand Lake and had no idea where it was.

I stumbled across a recent YouTube video on the subject of Hazel's death.[1] By midnight, still exhausted from illness, I had watched every video I could find and listened to every podcast on the subject up to that time. I found websites belonging to a handful of people interested in her murder. I had found all the stray news and magazine articles related to her death and the ghoulish "Halloween" stories from the New York papers recycling the story of Hazel's killing for a lurid thrill. Among these stories were many references to the disclosure by authors David Bushman and Mark Givens that Mark Frost, the co-creator of *Twin Peaks*, had heard stories of Hazel Drew from his grandmother Betty Calhoun, while spending time at her home near Sand Lake. Hazel's ghost allegedly haunted the woods around Teal's Pond, the site of her murder.[2]

I wondered, why wasn't Hazel's killing more famous?

The irony is that in 1908 Hazel's death was a sensation.

Every major American paper reported on Hazel Drew — whether reprinting wire service reports or actually sending reporters to Troy to cover the story. What emerged from that reportage and its regurgitation over the subsequent century is a settled narrative — The Legend of Hazel Drew.

However, as it turns out, the Legend isn't actually true. It's simple, it's elegant, and it ends with a satisfying mystery around which to speculate. Much of the tale was fictionalized by the tabloid press. Having reached that conclusion, I decided I would try my own hand at exploring Hazel's life and death. I felt justified, especially if her ghost had summoned us in a dream. That alone was befitting the murder that inspired *Twin Peaks*!

[1] Find a Grave (https://www.findagrave.com/memorial/36451324/hazel-irene-drew).

[2] "The Real Life Murder that Inspired the Show *Twin Peaks*: Hazel Irene Drew," Gabulosis, October 22, 2019, https://youtu.be/A31T_s38sow

[3] Bushman, David and Givens, Mark. "Hazel's Brutal Murder Was All But Forgotten...Until She Inspired *Twin Peaks*." *The Washington Post*, May 11, 2017.

THE LEGEND OF HAZEL DREW

CHAPTER 2

Hazel Irene Drew was born on June 3, 1888, to John and Julia Drew in Rensselaer County, New York. She was part of a large working-class family and was known locally for being outgoing and likable. She had a cadre of friends and relatives she was close to, particularly her aunt, Minnie Taylor, who was quite a bit older and single. Hazel attended church and had a busy social life for her era and station, at least outwardly.

Hazel moved to Troy at the age of 14, where she became a domestic servant in the homes of a series of prominent and wealthy community members. Hazel served as a governess, among the highest-status jobs in a home of this time period; she was entrusted with caring for the family's children. This was a big job for a teenage girl and, as such, Hazel must have cut a very professional and level-headed profile. By all accounts she was a popular and loved member of her social circle, though there was tension between her and her parents.

Hazel Drew was found dead on July 11, 1908, face down in a pond on the property of a farmer named Teal, miles from the home of her final employer in Troy. Initially the police and the local press thought the cause of death might have been suicide or an attempt to cover up an automobile accident. However, an autopsy soon revealed that Hazel died from blunt force trauma to the back of her head.

Hazel's death was the culmination of a week of uncharacteristically odd behavior. On the preceding Friday, July 3, Hazel arrived at the door of her dressmaker, Mrs. Schumacher at around 11:00pm begging her to make her a garment known as a shirtwaist for an Independence Day trip to the resort town of Lake George, New York. Hazel settled her standing debt with the tailor and was able to pay for the shirtwaist, a kind of blouse with billowy sleeves and a draw at the waist to enhance the figure. Mrs. Schumacher did the work, finishing the garment late at night. Hazel would be found dead in this same shirtwaist a week later.

According to friends and her aunt, Minnie Taylor, Hazel never made the trip to Lake George. Instead, she spent the weekend with her aunt and some cousins, and at the insistence of Ms. Taylor, returning to work on Monday, July 6. Hazel was hired by Professor Edward R. Cary and his wife Mary earlier in the year. Cary was an engineering professor at Rensselaer Polytechnic Institute. According to Mrs. Cary, she asked Hazel to do some laundry that Monday — perhaps not a normal task — and in response Hazel went upstairs, packed her trunk and suitcase, and quit work on the spot. Mrs. Cary told the local press she had no idea why she took that rash action; Hazel had been well-liked by the Carys.

From this point until her body was found, Hazel's whereabouts were fuzzy. Her trunk eventually appeared at her parents' house, where Hazel had it sent. After her death her suitcase was found checked at the local train station. At around 11:00am that Monday Hazel was spotted by a friend at the Troy Union Station. She told her friend she planned to head down the river. However, at 1:15pm Hazel was again seen at the station, this time without her suitcase. This means she would only have had time to take a fast trip to Albany and back.

Where Hazel spent the night of July 6th continues to be a mystery for many investigators. She was next seen some distance from Troy in the vicinity of the little hamlet of Sand Lake, overdressed in her new shirtwaist and skirt, carrying a black straw hat with three feathers in it, walking up Taborton Road in the direction of Teal's Pond. Her uncle William Taylor also lived off this road which had also previously been the home of Hazel's adult brother and sister-in-law. Hazel's younger brother was staying with a family that summer, also up Taborton Road in the direction of Teal's Pond.

Hazel herself was an infrequent visitor to her uncle's farm, but she had spent several weeks there recovering from an illness earlier in the year. Hazel Drew's presence on Taborton Mountain might seem odd, but it's not entirely an anomaly. She was from the area and had family there.

Hazel was witnessed by several locals as she made her steady walk up Taborton Road. A family spied her picking berries on the roadside. Among the last people to see Hazel was a local boy named Frank Smith, who exchanged brief words with her as he and an acquaintance rode by on a wagon. Frank was believed to have a crush on Hazel.

According to later witnesses, odd things were seen that night: mysterious automobiles and wagons in the area along with strange people appearing in Sand Lake. Regardless of what actually happened that night, Hazel was never seen alive again. Her body was recovered by a crowd of neighbors after being spotted in the water on July 11th.

The investigation into Hazel's death revealed almost immediately that like the dead heroine of *Twin Peaks*, she was living a double life. Yes, she was a churchgoer who always made her curfew, but far from being an innocent, when her trunk was recovered, it was found packed with correspondence from men, signing their names with initials to remain disguised. Among those was a letter from a man known only as C.E.S., who had sent her at least six letters. C.E.S. sent his letters from Boston and New York, cities Hazel had recently visited, and he made it clear that their relationship was steamy and possibly sexual. They had been meeting at an unnamed tavern in Albany.

*New York World, July 11, 1908. The heavily retouched photo
of Hazel Drew circulated in the Pulitzer papers, making
Hazel look older and more sexualized than she actually was,
contributing to her "legend."*

When Hazel's suitcase was found it contained a scandalous article of clothing: a silk kimono. It would appear that Hazel was a "good time girl" who, along with her aunt, spent time enjoying themselves in the company of men. Hazel dressed like an elite member of society, traveled, spent nights in luxury, dined at restaurants, and lived above her means.

Thus, many have surmised that Hazel was either getting gifts of cash from men as well as possibly engaging in sex work. This theory is buoyed by Hazel's extended stay with her uncle during the winter of 1908, due to a mysterious illness. Her parents never visited, and a doctor was never called. Rather she remained in the care of her sister-in-law.

She had to leave her employment as a result, as the client family could not go that long without domestic help. This has led many to conclude that Hazel was recovering from an abortion (highly illegal at the time), the truth of which would have destroyed her reputation. It was speculated that Hazel might even have been pregnant at the time of her death.

The police, under the direction of the local district attorney, would eventually investigate almost anyone who had even tertiary contact with Hazel in the months leading up to her death. These included her dentist and his son, a train conductor she may have had a friendship with, and even a local millionaire camp owner who the rumor mill accused of running some kind of sex club on his property. In the end, all these suspects proved to have alibis and were dismissed during a fruitless Coroner's inquest.

As the case stands, most theories of her murder revolve around Hazel planning to run away with a man, a plan that went sour, resulting in murder. A narrative has been established: Hazel Drew, gregarious and promiscuous, living large by trading her body for cash and gifts, became a victim of a lifestyle that caught up with her as she ran afoul of a dangerous man, a customer, or jealous suitor.

It's a simple narrative, perpetually recycled, that makes us feel like we almost have a solution to the case while still retaining an air of mystery. However, this narrative was the creation of the tabloid press and, as we will learn, of one particularly salacious writer named Will Clemens. In the pages that follow, I will argue that, rather than being on the make or some kind of cynical manipulator, Hazel was a good girl, who due to the behavior of others, got in over her head and wound-up dead. Her only sin was trusting others.

You've heard the Legend, now I'm going to tell you what really happened.

WELCOME TO
COLLAR CITY

CHAPTER 3

M rs. Montague was tired of doing laundry. She observed that her husband's shirts were only dirty at the collar and that it wasn't necessary to wash and iron the whole thing. Thus, she developed the practice of cutting her husband's collars off, washing them alone, and then stitching them back on. Today this seems ludicrous, but in 1825, before the invention of washing machines, doing laundry and ironing clothes was a difficult and even dangerous task. Mrs. Montague's frustration led to the invention of the detachable shirt collar, the clothing item that defined men's fashion for a century. Gone was the need to wash an entire shirt just to get at the dirty bits.

Troy, originally dubbed Ashley's Ferry, was given its new name in 1789, the year the United States Constitution was ratified. Thanks to Mrs. Montague, however, Troy earned itself the descriptive nickname "Collar City" a few decades later. Troy, in every sense of the word, is an American city. A garden spot along the Hudson, the Mohican and Skiwia natives were gradually cheated out of their lands by the wiles of Dutch Patroons and British settlers, beginning with the pearl and diamond trader Kiliaen Van Rensselaer, namesake of the present Rensselaer County.

Troy is so American, in fact, it is the literal home of our

national icon, Uncle Sam. Samuel Wilson, a meat packer, supplied American forces with victuals during the War of 1812. A city where "The Night Before Christmas" was initially published in 1823, to the location of the first Bessemer converter to be built in the United States, giving rise to the American steel industry, Troy played a leading role in the development of the culture and industry of the United States.

Troy's money came from steel and cloth. This innovation was heavily driven by the presence of Rensselaer Polytechnic Institute, established by a descendant of the founding patroon, Stephen Van Rensselaer. The school rests upon a geologic outcropping that overlooks Troy in the same way that the Parthenon overlooks the Greek city of Athens - apart from, yet integral to the community. The site of the school is unimaginatively called The Hill.

Because of the need for women workers in the garment industries, Troy became a city where women could work outside the home. Troy had a wide range of "working girls" including arguably the nation's most famous sex worker and madam, Mame Faye. Mame is said to have made so much money she had to lug it to the bank in duffel bags. She is famous for the quote: "Why work in a shop? Don't you know you're sittin' on a million?"

We cannot tell the story of Hazel Drew without understanding that Troy was the kind of city where women had above-average power and autonomy. It was a city where women in factory work, domestic work, and, yes, sex work had access to a higher standard of living than in many other American cities. Mame's brothel was right up the street from the police station and the cops stood guard at her place in exchange for free "coffee."

The sweatshop model took hold in Troy's factories. In 1864 Kate Mullany, only nineteen years old, convinced her co-workers to strike and form a union. Their collective action was a success and the world's first all-female labor union was born — the Collar Laundry Union. By the time Hazel Drew appeared on the scene, Troy was the kind of town where a single young woman could not only hold a job and be seen in public without a man, she could also form a labor union.[1]

It was into this maelstrom of rich and poor, steel and cloth that Hazel Drew was born. Clothes were important to Hazel. Clothes were important to Troy, New York. We must understand what they meant to the people of her era as a source of income, but also a reflection of one's status. The poorly dressed would be seen as poor and vice versa. Hazel Drew was compelled to visit her dressmaker late on a Friday night to purchase an expensive article of custom clothing that would set her apart from her peers as a woman capable of affording finery. Only days before Hazel died, she very much did not want to be seen as poor.

―――――

At the time Hazel Drew died modern scientific detection was in its infancy. No one person can be credited with inventing criminal detection, though the earliest to make an effort was likely Henry Fielding, a British magistrate. Fielding founded the first true investigative policing organization in the form of the Bow Street Runners, representing the Bow Street Magistrates Court in the City of Westminster, England. Fielding, of course, is more famously known as the author of the novel *Tom Jones*, solidifying the connection between the writerly mind and the detective.

Other forces emerged, from the municipal police under Eugène François Vidocq in Paris, to the mighty Scotland Yard in London. When Hazel died in 1908, Sherlock Holmes himself had only been introduced twenty-one years earlier by Sir Arthur Conan Doyle. At that time, both Washington, DC and New York City were in the process of modernizing their detective branches and the Federal Bureau of Investigation (FBI) was just getting started.

Law enforcement in Troy, New York was more akin to what we might find at Henry Fielding's magistrate court than what exists in that city today. Troy had a police department with a chief and officers and a couple of detectives and Rensselaer County had a sheriff with officers as well. The District Attorney — the officer charged with bringing cases to court to seek prosecution — had his own investigators coupled to the power to coordinate jurisdictions across city and town lines within the county. The County Coroner was the official who determined the cause of death and who could make early determinations regarding its circumstance as part of a public "inquest." Today a coroner is almost always a medical professional, and they make their determinations without a public inquest unless one is deemed relevant. In 1908, the coroner's inquest was almost like a grand jury investigation, except open to the public.

In 1908, in Upstate New York, virtually every public office was controlled at the whim of local politics. This was the era of the Political Bosses and Party Machines. To get any position of public trust in those days required either being elected or being wired to a boss or a politician who owed you spoils. The Troy-Albany region was under the sway of the powerful Republican Party. Still the party of Lincoln and a force for progressive values, New York City — coupled with its rival city Cleveland, Ohio — were the dominant forces in the United States during the post-Civil War Gilded Age.

Troy was a Republican city and more to it, Troy was an Irish city, specifically Irish Protestants. An increasingly persecuted minority in their homeland Irish Protestants melded easily into the cultural life of Upstate New York, once their accents had faded in the first and second generation. Hazel Drew, herself, was an Irish Protestant, by all accounts an extremely devout Methodist. Hazel wasn't a member of the elite, but she was a member of the local hegemony, and her murder represented the crossing of a line.

Striding through this miasma of machine politics, big money, and corruption at all levels was one man in particular, Jarvis P. O'Brien, the District Attorney. If anyone can be said to be the main character, though not the hero, of this tale, other than Hazel I. Drew herself, it's Jarvis O'Brien. Machine pol *par excellence*, he arose from a prominent political family in New

York, with a famous brother who had ties all the way to Theodore Roosevelt's White House. He was an academically trained lawyer, who spent most of his career representing and defending railroad tycoons (in no uncertain terms, absolute villains in 1908). His foray into politics was the result of his ties to the local Machine; he ran as a progressive reformer but continued the tradition of looking the other way at Mame Faye's brothel and handing jobs and perks to his buddies, among whom was his friend and loyal companion Duncan Kaye, who acted as the lead detective on the Drew case.

Topeka Daily State Journal, July 28 1908. Jarvis P. O'Brien, the District Attorney who led the investigation into Hazel's murder.

O'Brien was a Gilded Age lawyer. He might have known his way around a sketchy insurance policy or corporate indemnity clause, but he was not a criminologist. Nor were any of his investigators. His crew were spoilsmen and county office hangers-on. He perpetually surrounded himself with the press, often letting them look over clues his investigators had ignored and even allowing them to ask questions at the inquest. O'Brien was in charge of the case, but he was never in control of it. Spoiler Alert — O'Brien's failure to solve the Drew matter no doubt cost him his career in politics. But truth be told, even if he were totally motivated to solve the case, he was ill-equipped to do so. At times, in looking at his choices and deductions it is hard to differentiate between incompetence and intrigue.

[1] For a full exploration of industrial life in Gilded Age Troy, I recommend Carole Turbin's *Working Women of Collar City: Gender, Class, and Community in Troy, New York, 1864-86.* Champaign, University of Illinois Press, 1992.

HELLO, BEAUTIFUL
CHAPTER 4

T here was about six inches of snow on the ground when Eliza and I pulled my BMW up to the cemetery. It was a cold Upstate February, hovering well below freezing, the sky filled with steel grey clouds. The snow had been on the ground for days and was hardpacked and frozen. Even in good boots, walking around the untrodden cemetery was difficult.

Brookside Cemetery, where Hazel Drew is buried, on the day the author and friend first "met" her. Photo by the author.

We had no idea where the Drew family plot was located. We had seen photos of it online, taken in summer, but with no information about its location it would be a challenge to find. After an hour I was feeling cold and having stayed up almost all night putting together furniture for her new house, I was getting hungry and grouchy. My friend had given up the search and made her way to the biggest landmark at the cemetery: a gigantic native oak, around which there was no snowpack.

I wandered over to the tree, hoping to collect her and make our way to a diner for some food and hot coffee. I was ready to give up on the case. Some detective. I couldn't even find a grave in a cemetery.

"This tree is weird." My friend said, with a faraway look in her eyes. I was afraid the stress of staying up all night and home-buying was getting to her. "I touched it and now my hand feels like it was electrocuted!" she said, shaking it out and staring at her hand like it was no longer a part of her body.

"It's a creepy old tree and it's unusually warm under here," I said, as I approached it.

"I shouldn't have touched it," Eliza said, looking again at her hand. With the chill blowing and the clouds hanging low, the whole atmosphere got heavy, like kids playing with a Ouija board and nobody will admit to moving the planchette.

I don't know what I was thinking. Maybe I wasn't. It was as if something was calling me. Summoning me to the strange tree. I walked around to the opposite side she had touched and laid my hand on the tree's ancient, gnarled bark. I didn't feel a shock, but I immediately started to feel queasy. My first thought was the sleeplessness and excitement had me pumping too much cortisol. Holy shit, I thought to myself, I'm pushing fifty. Is this a heart attack?

My world started to spin, and I could feel the little bit of food and coffee I had in my guts churning and churning harder still. I was getting dizzy. I had to get away from that "witch" tree and maybe even get myself to a hospital. I hoped like hell that Eliza could drive my car—an ambulance wouldn't find us out there.

I started walking, then staggering, like I was about nine shots of whisky deep. The whole world was spinning. Finally, pouring cold sweat in that frozen landscape, my stomach gave up and I puked up pure liquid on the snow. I could see my friend's silhouette just staring back at me, unmoving. I kept pushing myself towards the car, but I'd lost the path. I was facing the wrong way now and I realized I was simply not going to make it. The ground rose up to meet me and I fell down, landing on my knees.

Getting on the ground, I caught my breath and managed to slow the spinning. My ungloved hands were resting on something cold and hard, and I looked down to see a single word carved in bone white marble: HAZEL.

Hazel Drew's tombstone. Photo by the author.

"I found it," I gasped, and my friend came running, whatever spell she was under, broken.

"Oh shit, oh shit, there it is! We were looking for an hour and there it is! Wait, are you ok?"

In fact, I was ok. Whatever spell I was under was also broken. My now empty stomach was still churning but my breathing was normal, and the world was no longer spinning. I looked back at the path I had taken, initially heading for my car but after vomiting, paradoxically taking a sharp turn to the right and collapsing on Hazel Drew's tombstone. Out of the hundreds of graves, I landed on her exact stone. What were the odds?

I was finally standing upright as Eliza approached the grave. This was the moment things took a turn from strange to outright spooky. Her eyes grew wide. I asked what was wrong. She said that she felt a tapping at the back of her head and was hearing a woman's voice yelling repeatedly "Like this! Like this!" as she floated behind her on the way to the grave. She described seeing a version of the murder as if from inside the body of Hazel Drew. I was simultaneously seeing the event from a bird's eye view.

That was strange enough, but both our spines ran up and

down with cold chills when we suddenly saw a well-dressed man in a loose-fitting spring suit approach, smiling.

"Did you just hear a man speak?" my friend whispered. "Yes!" I replied, flabbergasted. "He said, hello, beautiful," I said, barely believing the words coming out of my mouth. My friend nodded, speechless.

Thoroughly shaken, we snapped pictures of the area, including the path I followed to the grave, my footprints visible in the snow, collected ourselves, speaking few words, then drove in almost total silence to the closest diner. I ordered coffee, water, and a plate of eggplant parmesan. It was clear I wasn't going to die. We were both in a stupor and sat in our both, jackets still on, fiddling with menus and taking anxious sips of water, waiting on the coffee. Out of the blue, the murmuring cacophony of the restaurant was broken when a waitress passing by asked out loud, "Is Hazel coming?"

"Did you just hear that waitress say, 'Is Hazel coming?'" she asked me, her eyes wild again.

"Yes! I heard it too," I replied, feeling thoroughly spooked and confused. We were no longer in the graveyard. We were in a normal diner surrounded by the living, breathing, eating and drinking and talking, all of them seemingly oblivious of the clairaudient manifestation we had just experienced.

"What's happening?" Eliza asked, "How is this possible?"

I didn't have an answer. Frankly I still don't know what happened. Eliza and I continue to talk about that day just to remind ourselves that it wasn't a dream or a hallucination.

This was how we first met Hazel Irene Drew. It was only the beginning of the strangeness investigating this long-dormant cold case. Hazel was ready to reopen the files. She spoke, we heard her and could not ignore the story of a young woman robbed not only of her life but of her legacy.

MEET HAZEL DREW

CHAPTER 5

azel Drew rests in a bucolic cemetery nestled between two hillocks and surrounded by forest and farmland not terribly far from where her body was found at Teal's Pond. She is in the Brookside Cemetery, across Park Road from the Barberville Falls. The cemetery is close to where Blue Factory Road meets Plank Road. Hazel was born somewhere along Blue Factory, where, at the time, her family had a farm.

Much of Hazel's immediate family is buried alongside her now, though she was the first at Brookside. Her grave is made of white marble, worn from the elements, and is distinctive for having her name emblazoned on the top in all capital letters: HAZEL. Nearby stands a massive Northern Red Oak, the most prominent and by far the oldest tree in the immediate area.

If the anthropologists are to be believed, the ancient word for oak, *deru*, is the origin of Hazel's last name, which means "descendant of the Druids," the "oak-knowers" of Ireland's ancient past. This tree is perhaps a more fitting monument to Hazel than her unique tombstone. Oak. Drew.

Did Hazel know about her special connection to this mythic past? Did anyone in her family recognize the significance of her burial place? We cannot know. We know very little about Hazel Irene Drew beyond what she wanted the world to know. Like

Laura Palmer, the *Twin Peaks* character based upon her, she led a double life. The questions arise around the extent to which aspects of that second life may have led to her death.

Everyone said it, her aunt, her mother, her employers, her friends, and even the doctors who performed her autopsy: HAZEL WAS A GOOD GIRL. She never broke curfew and always came home at night. She never entertained male friends. She was such a devotee of the gospel that she regularly invited potential suitors on "dates" exclusively at church.

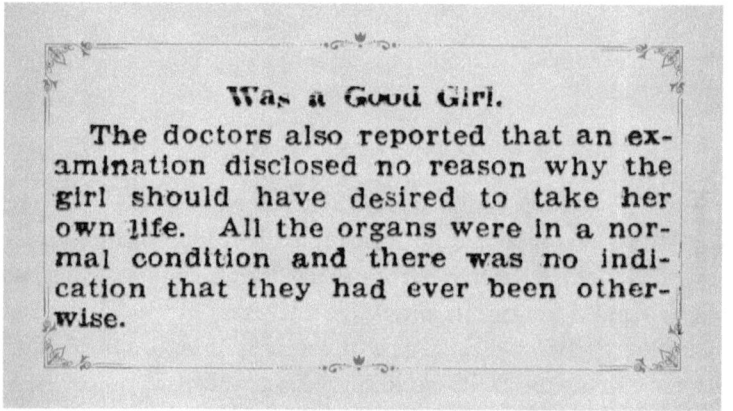

Was a Good Girl.
The doctors also reported that an examination disclosed no reason why the girl should have desired to take her own life. All the organs were in a normal condition and there was no indication that they had ever been otherwise.

Troy Daily Press, July 23, 1908. Everyone said it, even the doctors who performed her autopsy: Hazel Was a Good Girl.

Though her father was illiterate, Hazel liked to spend her free time reading. We do not know if she had any formal education, but her elocution, manners, and intellect were sufficient to allow her to be employed by a college professor. From what little we do know of Hazel she was very much a woman in command of her own affairs.

Hazel was born in what is today East Poestenkill in the vicinity of Blue Factory Road, named for an ancient business that produced a specific shade of Prussian Blue, integral to Troy's clothing industry. Though Hazel was born on a farm she would have been aware of industry and city life even at a very young age. Hazel could read and write and had access to the larger world through books. She lived close enough to Troy to be glamoured by city life, so it is not unreasonable to expect she would want to get off the farm as soon as possible.

Following Hazel's death, the press attempted to paint her relationship with her family as strained, if not outright estranged. But this appears not to have been the case for certain members of her extended family. She was close friends with her sister-in-law Eva and her aunt, Minnie Taylor (sister of Hazel's mother), herself a domestic in the grand houses of Troy, was her constant companion. According to accounts, Hazel's uncle William Taylor frequently took his young niece's advice.

Hazel's family were introverted and quiet people. Her Uncle Will battled depression and was referred to in the press as "morose" and "peculiar." Aunt Minnie acted shady throughout the investigation, engaging in a full-blown coverup. Hazel's mother often appeared unconcerned about her daughter's death.

Everything we know about Hazel points to her being a radically different type of person from her immediate family. She was fun-loving and extroverted rather than inward-looking and morose. Hazel was an ambitious and outgoing person in a family of somber introverts. The picture that emerges of Hazel Drew is that of a smart, gifted kid growing up in a family that was capable but considered odd by the standards of the day.

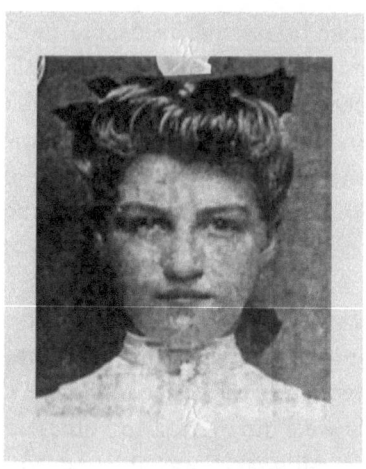

*Albany Times Union, July 14, 1908. Unretouched photo of
Hazel Drew, upon which the Pulitzer photo appears to be
based. Jarvis O'Brien reported to the press that this photo was
of Hazel when she was younger.*

At the age of 14, Hazel got her first job as a domestic servant.
A quick browse of contemporary newspapers indicates that on
any given day there were at least a dozen solicitations for women
and girls to work in domestic situations in Troy. These included
cooks, nannies, maids, both informal and formal, nurses, seam-
stresses, laundresses, and even women to sit and read to their
clients or play the piano.

We would expect Hazel Drew, as a novice domestic worker
barely in her teens, to begin her career on the lowest rung of the
servants' ladder, cleaning a lower middle-class house or doing
laundry all day. On the contrary Hazel's first job was at a stately
home at 360 Third Street in South Troy under the employ of
Thomas W. Hislop, Troy City Treasurer, member of all the most
influential local clubs, and powerful cog in the local Republican
Party machine.

There is nothing to confirm how Hazel got this job, but
Aunt Minnie probably helped. A Baltimore newspaper credited
Hazel's high-status jobs to her aunt, but this cannot be
confirmed. Aunt Minnie, herself, worked for the Troy elite and,
it's clear, knew people. We also can't count out the racism of the

political hegemony of the day. Hazel was a blond, blue-eyed Irish Methodist whom everyone stated was beautiful. Adding that she could read and write, she would be the perfect accouterment to a powerful man's home. Since Hazel herself was a member of that local hegemony, it would have been expected that anything she overheard that might be compromising, would be kept on the downlow.

Hazel took this first job in 1902, at a time when her family was living in Troy. In 1905 John moved the family to Taborton Mountain to the farm of Uncle William Taylor, to work as a sharecropper. Following a fight between the two men, the Drews were back in Troy by 1906. Throughout this tumultuous period Hazel continued to work in the city.

Hazel's longest period of employment was with Hislop, lasting until 1906. Thomas Hislop was everything we think of when we picture an American businessman of the late Victorian Era. Rather than falling into wealth or simply inheriting it, he was of that freshman class of the American professional that studied business as a vocation at the university. Born in Troy, he made enterprise his profession, with all the trappings, to include an eventual transition to public life.

Hislop's father owned a grocery store and it's clear, from an early day, he sought to go bigger. Hislop the younger was a veteran of the Spanish-American War and part of the National Guard and the local citizens regiments. He was a Mason and an Elk. He was in so good with the local pastor of the Third Street Methodist Church, that at one point that preacher was living in the Hislop home.

Hislop owned the Troy and West Troy Ferry—one of the arteries that brought goods and people across the mighty Hudson. He also managed a glass company called Foot and Thorn. At the time Hazel joined the Hislops' employment, the household consisted of Thomas, his wife Nellie, and their children Mabel and Thomas Jr., as well as the aforementioned pastor, John M. Harris. If there was a pie baking in Troy, Thomas Hislop had his finger in it.

Hislop entered politics at a time when municipal offices were becoming professionalized. He was easily elected to the office of Treasurer and was subsequently re-elected. However, Hislop's ambition got the better of him. Getting ahead of himself in the order of party seniority, Hislop threw his hat in the ring, running for mayor of Troy as a third-party candidate on the Citizens Party ticket. Though he had the backing of local political royal Albert C. Comstock, he was doomed. Turning his back on the Grand Old Party cost him the race and he came in third, behind the two establishment candidates. Republican Elias Plum Mann became mayor and Thomas W. Hislop was out of office for the rest of his life.

There were further consequences. Following the falling out with the local GOP, Hislop's Deputy got caught with his hand literally in the till and was convicted of stealing $10,000 from the city. The city eventually sued Hislop to recover the funds. We can imagine that if Hislop had stayed on the Machine's good side, none of this unpleasantness would have occurred. New York machine politicians were as thick as thieves—because they were often literally thieves. Hislop's betrayal was swiftly punished.

As this chaos and controversy played out, Hazel Drew was working in the Hislop home, leaving in 1907, the reason publicly unknown. She did not take a downgrade with her next position, however, landing at 711 Fulton Street, at the home of coal magnate John H. Tupper. No doubt the Tuppers and Hislops were friends, both John and Thomas were prominent members of the Republican Machine, and both were members of the local Troy Citizens Corp and National Guard. Tupper was a union-busting coal man who had himself lost the position of mayor ten years earlier to a Democrat.

———

Hazel's new home sat in a curious part of Troy, near where the Uncle Sam Lanes bowling alley is today. It was close to the Troy Union Station and the Police Station, but also immediately adjacent to Mame Faye's notorious stomping grounds and the string of hotels and brothels that made up Troy's Redlight District. We are reminded of the extent to which sex work was fully integrated into Troy society.

Much like her hiring by Hislop we do not know how Hazel came to work for the Tuppers, though we can speculate. She was particularly close to Mrs. Adelaide Tupper, retaining a friendship after she left their employment. It is likely she knew Mrs. Tupper before going to work for her due to contact between the two families. Mrs. Tupper, following a trip to Canada, where she was from, gifted Hazel with the brooch she was wearing when she was found floating in Teal's Pond. It bore the coat of arms of the city of Montreal (something most authors and commentators have failed to discern) and read *Concordia Salus*, "salvation through harmony." The brooch contained Hazel's initials, HID, and was apparently a prized piece of jewelry.

Hazel's illness in the winter of 1908 was the event that caused Hazel to separate from the Tupper residence. Having fallen ill on Christmas Day 1907 and requiring assistance in her work from her Aunt Minnie, Hazel would eventually spend about three weeks recuperating at her Uncle William Taylor's Taborton Mountain farm. Though her parents lived nearby on Fourth Street in Troy at this time, she seems to have chosen the farm because her brother Joseph and sister-in-law Eva, one of Hazel's best friends, were living there. Clearly this is where she thought she could get the care she needed to recover.

While at the Taylor farm John Tupper fired Hazel by postage, sending her a severance letter and money in the mail. Just like that, he'd found another servant and Hazel would have to find another job. This, however, turned out not to be a problem. Almost immediately she was hired to work as a governess in the home of, of course, another prominent member of the local Republican establishment, Edward Richard Cary, a professor at RPI. Hazel went to work for him almost immediately.

Cary was a civil engineer who, like her previous bosses, wore many hats. He became a professor in the Engineering Department of Rensselaer Polytechnic almost immediately upon graduation and established a personal precedent of holding that position while engaged in private enterprise. Throughout his career he had a wide range of business interests beyond academics.

I have been able to establish that he was a partner in an engineering firm, a designer of sections of the local and regional trolly car system, a builder (possibly in partnership with family members), the architect of much of the city's water management plan, and, of course, at times the Troy City Engineer and engineer for the towns of Green Island and Watervliet as well as a consulting engineer to a number of cities and railroads. Cary's academic appointment seems to have changed and evolved throughout his long career at RPI, but he was primarily the Professor of Geodesy—the field of mathematics related to the shape of the earth.

Essentially, he was a surveyor, eventually publishing a book on that topic. Professor Cary would retire from RPI after a forty-eight-year career, as the chair of the Department of Geodesy and Railroad Engineering. Trains were the man's passion, and he spent his retirement years working on various railroad projects in South Carolina, where he and his wife passed away. Cary Hall on the RPI campus is named for him.

Cary, like all of Hazel's employers, found himself in a hell of a mess right around the time Hazel was in his employment. The same financial shenanigans that seemed to haunt the early twentieth-century officeholders of Troy also plagued the City Engineer's office. Cary was passing spoils and patronage to relatives and, frankly, had too many jobs going on at once to give any of them his full attention. Court documents reveal that his engineering skills were at least once called into question, as the steep grade of a track bed was alleged to have caused a car to lose control, resulting in a death.

Cary was not a politician, though he was heavily connected to the local GOP establishment and the political machine, his family being prominent and of long-standing. Cary married well, was well connected, and, by all appearances, quite well off. We do not associate the profession of college professor with wealth today, but in Cary's time it was a job *for* the wealthy, not one that would lead to wealth on its own. Obtaining a good education with the time to dabble in academics was for the elite, prior to the G.I. Bill and the student grant and loan programs that emerged following World War II. Cary, however, seemed to be extraordinarily committed to the hustle, attempting to parlay his professor status into as much extra-curricular paid work as possible. Even following his exit as City Engineer, he continued to perform work for the city, for the Town of Green Island, and for an array of companies and investors, to the point that it is hard to establish just how wide his network of business connections ran.

Hazel Drew worked for the Carys for just about five months, when she—according to Mrs. Cary—walked off the job and into eternity in early July 1908. It was during this period that Hazel enjoyed the most prosperous period of her short life. She enjoyed trips to Boston, Providence, and New York City, as well as the fine meals and clothes spoken of so heavily in the press after her murder. Whether it was the Carys themselves or via some other patron, Hazel came into a decent income at this time and the Carys seemed to afford her the days off to make a number of trips, though she was a brand-new employee.

It was also at this time, during the last few months of her life, that Hazel began to pull away from her friends and contacts. Other authors and the investigators in 1908 have failed to make this observation, which we will discuss later. Though Hazel was "getting out" more, she was shrinking her network and list of contacts.

Edward and Mary Cary were living in a new house on Whitman Court, to this day one of the prettiest and most fashionable streets in Troy, when Hazel went to work for them. She was hired as the governess for their eleven-year-old daughter Helen, who appears to have lived to the ripe old age of 89 without ever speaking publicly about Hazel Drew's death. Doubtless no one ever asked her. Helen would have been the only intimate of Hazel Drew who was old enough to remember her last days that could provide the modern researcher with any insight. She died in 1986, a handful of years before *Twin Peaks* hit the airwaves, and interest in Hazel began to be revived.

We have met Hazel Drew, recounting literally everything we know about her from the historic record, up to February of 1908. The last five months of her life—about which we know considerably more—will fill out the remainder of this book. It is a difficult story to tell in an orderly and coherent narrative for, like *Twin Peaks* itself there are many side stories that have to be told for the overall story to make any kind of sense. So let's take a moment and dive into those, one by one, to help us better understand what was going on in Hazel Drew's life and how confusing it was to unravel this mystery.

PART TWO
INCIDENTS & INDIVIDUALS

BILLY BROWN

CHAPTER 6

O ne of the puzzling aspects of Hazel Drew's murder is why it was such an all-consuming media event for that one hot month of July 1908. Not to sound too dismissive of the tragedy, but a lot of people got killed in the early twentieth century without their deaths becoming a sensation. We do not have good crime figures, but we do know that it was significant to the point that there was public outcry for more professionalized policing and politicians who were running for office on exactly these reforms. As I did the research for this book, skimming through digitized newspapers and microfilm, the report of some brutal murder totally unconnected to Hazel's death would catch my eye and provide a temporary distraction. None of these caught fire the way Hazel's death did. Why?

Billy Brown.

The striking similarities between Hazel Drew's death and that of Grace "Billy" Brown, whose shocking murder by a member of a prominent New York family, captivated the world only two years earlier. *Exactly* two years to the day that Hazel Drew's body was found in Teal's Pond, on July 11, 1906, another working-class girl, Grace Brown—known as Billy due to her love of the song "Won't You Come Home Bill Bailey"—was taken out onto Big Moose Lake in Upstate New York and clobbered over the head with a tennis racket or a boat oar. Following the attack, she either fell into the water or was pushed, where she then drowned.

TROY'S MYSTERIOUS TRAGEDY

Police Hunting for the Murderers of a Pretty Girl Whose Body Was Fund Floating In a Pond

Troy, N. Y., July 17.—Rivaling in mystery and horrible detail the killing of Grace Brown, at Big Moose Lake, for which crime Chester Gillette paid the penalty in the electric chair, is the murder of Miss Hazel Drew, the pretty 18-year-old daughter of John Drew of this city, which is being proved by the police now.

Ocala Evening Star, July 17, 1908. The press immediately associated Hazel's murder with the death of Billy Brown.

Like Hazel, Billy was twenty years old. She was also a prolific letter writer, writing a number of love letters which she signed "The Kid," taken from her nickname and that of Billy the Kid. Unlike Hazel, Billy seems not to have been in charge of her life and was very much in the thrall of a more powerful man who used her up—a certain Chester Gillette.

Gillette was a young man only a couple of years older than Billy and what would have been called a "wastrel" in his day. He came from a good upper-crust family, but never managed to get his life together. His parents were rich, but they renounced that lifestyle to work and travel with the Salvation Army. Unlike his parents, Chester never took to religion. He survived on the benevolence of relatives. One of his uncles got him into prep school, though he dropped out, ending his education. He bummed around and worked odd jobs until going to work for a fraternal uncle at the Gillette Skirt Factory in Cortland, New York.

It was at this factory where he met Billy Brown, who had also recently started working there. Unlike Hazel's chaste church dates and intimations of heavy petting, Billy and Chester's relationship was overtly and immediately sexual, with Billy documenting it in a series of love letters. Chester was a good-looking man, more than handsome by the standards of his day, with angular features and a cleft chin. He would have been a good catch—had he wanted to be caught.

The relationship was rocky, after a fashion, with acquaintances noticing arguments as it progressed. There were even later accusations that Chester was only toying with Billy while trying to bag a rich woman for himself which, frankly, seems in character. Nevertheless, by early 1906 Billy was pregnant, and Chester was faced with a limited slate of choices. The honorable thing to do would be to marry his lover and, at the very least, try to be a decent provider. We know from her surviving letters that this was the path Billy preferred. Chester could have also chosen to pay for an abortion, which at least wouldn't saddle Billy with the burden of a child, though the practice was highly illegal. But instead of choosing either extremity, he instead decided to murder her. It reads like a seedy noir plot. Real life is truly stranger than fiction.[1]

We aren't exactly sure what Chester told Billy to get her to go on the road with him. It was a proposed trip to the Adirondack Mountains. Gillette seems to have promised her marriage, though it has been argued by more recent investigators that he may have promised to take her to a maternity home where she could deliver the child. Regardless, his behavior was highly suspect, which Billy either never noticed or ignored. For instance, Billy took her entire wardrobe with her—while Chester only packed a small suitcase for himself. Odd for a man running off to start a newly married life. They also traveled incognito, checking into hotels under assumed names and, at one point, skipping out on a hotel bill.

The couple planned a boat outing on Tupper Lake, but rain spoiled their fun. This may have been where Chester initially planned to kill Billy. With the game called due to weather, the couple found themselves rowing into Big Moose Lake on July 11, 1906—about 150 miles north of Teal's Pond. The events of that outing are unknown. Gillette either hit her with the tennis racket strapped to his suitcase or a boat oar and Billy either fell into the water or was pushed, with her cause of death ultimately due to drowning.

Billy's body was found the next day and Chester was arrested almost immediately, as witnesses had seen the couple rowing out into the lake. Chester Gillette was both a villain and a fool, claiming that Billy was distraught and had simply jumped into the water on her own accord. Chester claimed he tried to save her, himself falling into the water, but he didn't tell anyone about the incident after getting back to shore, so that story didn't wash. Chester's rich uncle, obviously scandalized, refused to pay for a defense team and the young man was forced to mount his idiotic defense via a public attorney. Chester sold photos of himself to onlookers from jail so he could buy fancy hotel meals while locked up. Priorities, right?

After a whirlwind prosecution, the jury barely got out of their seats to make their decision, and on December 4th, 1906, they found Gillette guilty of murder in the highest degree. Governor Charles Evans Hughes—a guy with a brass set so big he took on and defeated William Randolph Hearst for the office in 1906—saw no reason to stick his neck out for Chester Gillette and let the death sentence stand without granting clemency. On March 30, 1908, Chester Ellsworth Gillette was electrocuted to death at Auburn Prison. He was 24 years old.

The media of 1906 was captivated by the Billy Brown murder and by Gillette himself. In the Gilded Age, the story of the rich man murdering his working girl employee was ripped right from the pages of popular fiction. The small-town setting, though still close to the media center of New York City, made it an easy case to cover. There was sex and tragedy, and Gillette was just the kind of fool who seemed to adore the attention which, in the end, other than buying him high-class meals, did him no good.

Grace Brown left behind a mountain of letters, many of which were removed from Gillette's room when he was arrested. These were read into court documents during the trial while others were quickly published and literally sold on the court-house steps to the prurient crowd and journos. The story was as hot as the summer weather and became a nationwide sensation. Gillette's execution, which came with desperate pleas for redemption, brought the whole thing back into the news just four months before Hazel herself died.

The papers, yellow as they were, immediately attempted to link Hazel and Billy. On July 13, 1908, the *Evening Statesman* way out in Walla Walla, Washington invoked the death of Grace Brown to put Hazel Drew on the front page. Scotland, South Dakota, Ocala, Florida, Perth Amboy, New Jersey, and of course, in Troy, itself, from the four corners of the United States, news-papermen seemed to salivate over Hazel Drew's murder, bringing them the kind of sales they'd received covering Brown and Gillette.

It was both natural and disgusting that the men who made money selling American tragedies would look to Hazel Drew as their next market. This explains why her case was so immediately popular. It was a welcome, if sorrowful, antidote to the all-compelling politics filling the news. That same Walla Walla paper put Hazel Drew and Billy Brown right alongside William Jennings Bryan, the man they wanted in the White House, on that front page.

In one final note of eerie coincidence, that Chester Gillette's last letter, before his date with Thomas Edison's electric chair, was written to his sister—whose name happened to be Hazel.

---

[1] The tragedy of Billy Brown inspired a wide range of pop culture creations, beginning with Theodore Dreiser's landmark 1925 novel, *An American Tragedy*. Dreiser's novel itself was adapted into plays, radio broadcasts, and television productions.

But the most famous direct adaptation was the 1951 George Stevens film *A Place in the Sun*, which captured six Academy Awards. Based on Dreiser's novel and the real story of Brown, Charlie Chaplin called it "the greatest film made about America."

SLITERS CORNERS

CHAPTER 7

W here did Hazel Drew die? Hazel Drew's body was found in a pond connected at a distance to a sawmill owned by farmer Conrad "Coon" Teal.

Teal's Pond is a manmade body of water sitting near the headwaters of a shallow but lively creek that eventually flows into the larger Wynantskill below its headwaters at Glass Lake. You will not find Teal's Pond listed on any map as such. It is near the apex of Taborton Mountain on the Taborton Road just beyond the southward turn before Roaser Road. It is on private property today and was on private property when Hazel Drew went there in 1908.

In 1908 Teal's Pond was a lively spot that old Coon Teal did not try very hard to police. News reports indicate that people stopped there often to catch baitfish for fishing, a camp of young rowdies was nearby, and a lot of hunting, fishing, and carousing got done in the area, which Mr. Teal was both aware and permissive of. Perhaps he got up to it as well. As we will learn, heavy traffic along Taborton Road in 1908 confounds this mystery even further. Thus, it is keenly important we have a precise understanding of the setting.

When referring to the place where Hazel traveled to and died in 1908, most writers and researchers refer to it either as the

Town of Sand Lake or Averill Park, or they simply use these place names interchangeably. However, most of the "action" during Hazel's last moments took place in and around an area of Sand Lake that is known as Sliters Corners, which sits at the intersection of Miller Hill Road and Taborton Road.

Sand Lake has quite an ancient story, dating well back into Native American history. Kiliaen van Rensselaer, director of the Dutch West India Company, established the Manor of Rensselaerswyck in 1630 consisting of over a million acres of land encompassing what is today the New York Capital Region. Important to our story, James K. Averill established the Troy and New England Railway Company in 1895. It provided an electric trolly service between Averill Park and a station at Albia, just inside Troy's city limits. It was James K.'s intention to eventually connect this line to Pittsfield, Massachusetts, hence the addition of "New England" to the company's name. That extension never happened and by 1925 the line was defunct.

It was this "Albia car" that Hazel Drew would have used to get to Averill Park in 1908. These old cars were primitive—even more so than what we might think of when we envision the Rice-A-Roni streetcar or *A Streetcar Named Desire*. Think, essentially, a four-wheeled wagon—open in the summer and closed in winter—rolling on a narrow gauge, rough laid piece of track, with sparking exposed electrics. By 1908 the city of Troy was positively congested with these things, as old photos show, and their cost and inconvenience eventually had them supplanted by automobiles.

In Hazel's day, the Averill Park Station was located on Orient Avenue in what was then the center of town. From old photographs we can see it was a primitive affair, a tiny building with an overhang just big enough to cover one of the tracks. Its last purpose before being demolished was as a warehouse for a lumber company. The site today is easy enough to find— nothing has been built there and it remains an open lot. If one looks carefully, it is easy to see how the tracks once ran, the open beds still serve as a kind of easement around Averill Park and Sand Lake at large.

To get to this last stop on the line, Hazel Drew would have had to take connecting trolleys in Troy and walk a little bit to get to the Albia Station. These old trolleys did not function as modern public transportation does. They were independently owned and competing lines that often did not offer connections or ticket transfers. One paid a fee to ride to one station, got off, went to another station, and paid another company's fee to ride further on. This was also true for the main steam rail line that ran through Troy. It was a private railroad that connected to trains headed further south across the river in Albany.

A Number 3 city trolley car would have taken Hazel to the end of that line, near a landmark called the Terminal Tavern. The old tavern has long since closed, but the building, as of this writing, still stands, and is a glimpse into what passed for a drinking establishment in Troy more than one hundred years ago. Hazel would then walk a block or so to the Troy and New England Albia Station, which stood at about where Route 66 takes a bend in the road today. Many landmarks from that era have been erased due to development. From the Albia Station she would travel on to Averill Park roughly following Route 150 southward, with stops along the way.

The Averill Park terminus sat in what is today a residential part of Sand Lake. In those days it would have had more of a "main street" feel with a few little hotels and boarding houses interspersed among the old Victorian and newer Edwardian homes. Averill Park was trying to boost itself as a kind of second Coney Island, known for its sandy lake beaches. Hot July, when Hazel made her last call, was their high season.

Hazel would have had a choice to make in Averill Park in trying to get to Taborton Mountain. She could have headed north up Orient to the "main drag" of Old 66 and then east past Young's Pharmacy, a landmark that is still around. Or she could have meandered east around the station, crossing Burden Lake Road and entering Tin Pan Alley, taking a scenic route past the lake. Either way, she would eventually be forced to funnel into the little community of Sliters Corners at the crossroads. Following on from Sliters Corners, there was a steep ascent up Taborton Road, approaching a

bend at that time called Taylor's Turn. To the north of the turn lay
her uncle William Taylor's farm, to the south was Teal's Pond.

The primary feature of Sliters Corners in 1908 was the
Central Hotel, owned at the time by Chris (also spelled Crist)
Crape. In the news accounts from Hazel's day, it was typically
just called "Crape's Hotel." Sliters Corners was named for the
Sliter family, early settlers. Clement Sliter may have once oper-
ated the tavern that became the Central Hotel.

Local lore states that the place was built around 1800 and
became a popular stagecoach stop. It was owned by John
Stephens until 1830 when it was sold to James Gill Averill, who
married Clement Sliter's daughter, parents of the two gents who
would literally put Averill Park on the map, Horatio and James.
One reference from 1880 stated the hotel was already at least 60
years old at the time of that writing. The building went through
numerous changes, finally ending its life as a private residence
before being demolished in 1957.

In 1908 Mr. Crape was running his hotel in a white two-
story wooden structure with sizeable building-length porches on
the first and second floors. A photo from 1910 at the Sand Lake
Town Historian's Office shows a hammock hung out on one of
these porches on the second floor, a bunch of folks relaxing
outside, and even a friendly old dog hanging out in the yard.
This is what Hazel would have seen walking by the place on her
last afternoon.

The hotel was located on the southeast corner of Miller Hill
Road and Taborton Road. There is a lot of confusion about this
location among researchers but a careful study of period maps
and newspaper articles from the time of the demolition confirms
the site. It is key to understanding Hazel's last movements. The
structure was demolished in 1957 to make room for a gas
station, which has subsequently been transformed into a used
car lot. Sliters still has an excellent tavern, today situated behind
the former location of Crape's Hotel.

The roads that intersect at the heart of Sliters Corners have
changed since 1908—enough to make the geography confusing.

Chris Crape had a bigger piece of real estate than exists today, with a few elms out front surrounded by a white picket fence. The place sat back from the road further than the property on which the car lot now rests, giving some distance between the hotel and the old Taborton Road, which was narrow and dirt in 1908.

Averill Park was a resort town, thus it boasted a lot of hotels. Crape's was a good distance east of the station and the tourist sites that post-dated it, as it had been built at an ancient crossroads rather than oriented around the modern trolley station. From reports in old newspapers, it must have been a rowdy place. Frank Smith, among the last to see Hazel Drew alive, finished his evening there the night she was killed, engaged in a wild drinking and wagering party that ran very late. That day was a *Tuesday*, so Mr. Crape did not mind partying hard on any given night.

It appears from reports that he sat up on his porches very late into the night watching the comings and goings. Crape's was a spot where locals went to use the new-fangled telephone, take baths, and get shaves and haircuts. William Taylor headed up there for a shave the day Hazel's body was found. Crape ran a restaurant that often sat up to a hundred people at Sunday supper, which he and his family victualed with produce and meats from their own garden.

A picture of Crape's hotel emerges. Party central, gossip central, and a true hangout for the "locals," Crape's Hotel was a hub around which life in eastern Sand Lake rotated. The fact that so little intelligence about Hazel Drew's last moments was obtained by the hotelier and his guests is of interest, as we will explore.

In setting the geography of Hazel Drew's last moments I must draw attention to one other confusing landmark. This is the site of "Brown's Hotel." This structure is most properly known as the Wendell Inn, located further south on Miller Hill Road at Crooked Lake. In 1908 it was owned by the local Brown family and was often referred to simply as "Brown's Hotel"—in much the same way the Central Hotel was referred to as "Crape's Hotel."

This is important, because according to his own account Frank Smith, on the night Hazel Drew died departed from a meeting at "Brown's" to discuss work and headed into Averill Park, where, along the road, he was one of the last witnesses to see Hazel Drew alive. Researchers have confused the Brown of Frank Smith's account with Brown's Hotel, which cannot be the case. In fact, Frank Smith was departing from a farm on Taborton Mountain owned by a "Brown" and headed down Taborton Road, not from the hotel further south and in the opposite direction.

Taborton is, itself, both a mountain and a small village located on that mountain, beyond Teal's Pond further to the east.

In a later chapter we will build a meticulous timeline of Hazel's movements during her last weekend. To accomplish that, a solid understanding of the geography of those movements is important. In Hazel's day this geography was more regimented and distinct. Understanding the lay of the land will help us unravel the mystery.

Dear Old Aunt Minnie

Chapter 8

Though Hazel Drew's Aunt Minnie lived a long life, we know very little about her — and we certainly don't know enough to feel satisfied. Whatever she was, she was the person who was the closest to Hazel Drew in the last months of her life. Hazel had been drawing her circle closer in those last few months and Minnie was a big part of her life in the end. If Minnie did not know who Hazel's killer was, then her behavior demonstrates that she certainly had a suspicion. Minnie behaved like a person who knew things. Considering how her life changed after Hazel Drew's death I believe there is good evidence for this.

The Taylor clan was a large family, as nineteenth century farming families often were. The head of the Taylor household, Charles William Taylor, Sr., was born in 1827, and Mary Ann Taylor, *née* Lapp, born in 1824. Records indicate that Charles was born in either "Baden" or Hanover, Germany, with Mary from Hesse-Kassel, Germany. Minnie Taylor was the next to youngest of their children, with sister Amelia being about two years younger and William Taylor being about sixteen years her senior. We say "about" here because Minnie and her family were not clear on her birthday. In the 1870 census Minnie was listed as being born "about 1868" at the age of 2 years. The 1880 census — and in all other documents going forward — she is listed as being born "about 1869." No actual Month/Day is ever given for her birth, including on her tombstone.

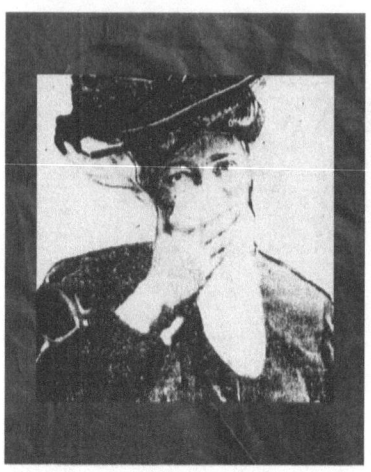

New York World, July 16, 1908. Hazel Drew's Aunt and close confidant, Minnie Taylor.

All the Taylor children were born in the United States with the family as a whole living, at times, in both Berlin and Poestenkill, New York. Charles Sr. died in 1878, with Mary following in 1897. Hazel Drew would have been just old enough to have some memory of her grandmother Taylor.

Minnie Taylor had an eighth-grade education which means, like Hazel, she would have known how to read and write. Her full name was most often listed simply as "Minnie Taylor," though she may have had a middle name that began with the letter "C" or a "K" as some records indicate. With Charles Senior's passing in 1878, by the 1880 census the eleven-year-old Minnie was already working at an adult job making shirts in Poestenkill, likely in one of the factories. The employment of child labor in mills during the nineteenth century was a common practice. Her eventual career performing domestic work for the Great and the Good would be a huge step up in life.

By 1908 Minnie was somewhere around the age of 38 or 39

— or possibly she had already turned 40 by the time Hazel was murdered. The newspapers portray her in the classic trope of the "maiden aunt" with all the unspoken implications regarding her sexuality. There are a handful of photographs of Minnie Taylor in the old newspapers and in some family papers I have seen. To say she looked fierce is an understatement — she had a prominent nose, set jaw, and piercing intelligent eyes.

We don't know exactly how Minnie got to Troy in the employ of the city's elite. The historical record leaves only a few clues. She was doing housekeeping work in the 1880's in the Troy suburb of Lansingburgh. She also worked for a time as a housekeeper in Lansingburgh's Phoenix Hotel, a hangout for the locally well-connected. Minnie appears to have closed out the nineteenth century in Greenfield, Massachusetts near her older sister Mary Ann and her family.

Through whatever connections she had made, possibly while working at the Phoenix, popular with the local Republican establishment, by 1905 Minnie Taylor was in the employ of local robber baron George B. Harrison, who owned a sizeable mansion on Pawling Avenue, near the Carys' at Whitman Court. Hazel was able to skip over the more menial stages of work life that Minnie endured, no doubt through Minnie's own connections. It is near certain that Minnie Taylor was Hazel's entrance into this world, as the connections are obvious. For instance, both Tupper and Hislop, Hazel's bosses before Professor Cary, were members of the Troy Citizens Corps, alongside Harrison. Of course, they were all prominent members of the GOP.

Despite an age difference of some eighteen to twenty years, aunt and niece were clearly great friends. Minnie was furiously devoted to her family. For example, she once took legal action to prevent her sister's widowed husband from getting his hands on a chunk of the profit from her parents' farm. Throughout her life Minnie would spend a lot of time in the company of her relatives — cousins, nieces, and nephews. Though she seemed to have an especial fondness for Hazel. Minnie reported to the press and to investigators that she saw Hazel as many as three nights per week with Hazel often staying over with her at the Harrison house.

George B. Harrison was a man of inherited wealth — his father had owned the venerable Troy Malleable Iron Works. Harrison the younger lined up all the credentials required to turn a fortune into a bigger fortune in the Gilded Age. He was an attorney, banker, and real estate developer. The only pieces of the Monopoly board he lacked were a few railroads and the waterworks. And, hell, for all we know he probably had shares in those.

Harrison's house was large enough — and he was generous enough — to allow Hazel Drew to stay with her aunt, on the regular, essentially while she was on the job. This seems to fit with what little we know of Harrison's character. His legacy, rather than one of business and commerce, along the lines of his father, is that of a man who enjoyed spending time being "well-clubbed;" he loved to socialize. This further leads us to conclude that he was likely the source of the connections — through Aunt Minnie — that got Hazel her series of good jobs.

Minnie Taylor, if her account is to be believed, spent Hazel's last weekend alongside her. It was Hazel's intention to go to Lake George for Independence Day, thus the need for Hazel to stay up all night for the infamous custom shirtwaist. However, Minnie allegedly talked her out of the trip and instead the duo went to spend time with family in Schenectady. A trip, notably, for which Hazel would not need fancy clothes.

By Minnie's own admission she was the person with whom Hazel spent the most time. Also, by her own admission, she had knowledge of the people who were close to Hazel in her life — the people with whom she spent leisure time and the people she was meeting on her travels to Boston, Providence, and New York. However, Minnie adamantly dug in her heels and refused to provide this crucial information to O'Brien and the other investigators. Right up until the inquest, she simply refused to cooperate by providing useful assistance. Minnie was engaged in a cover-up.

On July 18, 1908, O'Brien brought Minnie "downtown" to

"sweat" her to try to get information out of her. The investigators had some evidence that Hazel and another woman — likely Minnie — had been seen riding around Averill Park with unknown men. O'Brien wanted to know about the people in Hazel's life so he could track down leads. The proceedings went roughly; Minnie cried and went faint, and stimulants were applied to keep her going. The *Evening World* of that day stated dramatically "Aunt of Hazel Drew Collapses Under Third Degree..."

At this interview Minnie was questioned by O'Brien and two officers, Kaye and Murnane, the D.A.'s own loyal lieutenants. Despite the fainting couch drama, Aunt Minnie gave up a couple of names of Hazel's associates, including the men seen with the ladies in Averill Park, none of which turned out to be real leads. Rather, on the way out of the courthouse Aunt Minnie told the assembled press: "Don't bring innocent persons into this terrible affair."

But how did Aunt Minnie know who was innocent unless she knew who was guilty?

Minnie Taylor took this cover-up a step further. She contacted Hazel Drew's closest and oldest friend, Mrs. Mina Jones, who was living in Waterville, Maine, and asked her to destroy any letters she had between herself and Hazel. This was reported on July 22nd in the *Troy Times*. Mrs. Mina Jones, who clearly knew both Hazel and Minnie very well, reported upon inquiry that Minnie had written to her and asked her to destroy her correspondence. Mina was reluctant and informed Minnie she was planning to keep three recent letters and six postcards from Hazel, none of which contained anything that "could hurt her or anyone else."

At no point was Minnie Taylor ever made to divulge what she knew, what she was trying to cover up, or what potential persons could have been mentioned in those letters. Mina Jones did admit that several of her letters from Hazel had been destroyed during a recent move from Providence, Rhode Island to Maine. A move Mrs. Jones was decidedly unhappy about.

What is so annoying about Minnie Taylor is that she clearly

knew something and had a strong suspicion who the killer was, but she got away with never being made to talk. The D.A. and the investigators never could get a middle-aged domestic to say a damn word. It leads one to believe that they actually never intended to try that hard. They could have arrested her on all manner of charges, from withholding evidence to perjury. This was before the Miranda Ruling - they could have tossed Minnie in the lockup for as long as they wanted.

Except, of course, she worked for George B. Harrison. She was a friend of the Tuppers and a friend of the Hislops and one giant listening ear at the GOP-loved Phoenix Hotel and in one of the most powerful houses in Troy. O'Brien ran the very real risk that if Minnie Taylor started talking about people, she might not decide to shut up.

We know O'Brien did not take questioning Minnie seriously. Despite the pretense of the "sweat" at which only GOP loyalists were present, at the actual public inquest O'Brien passed on asking Minnie hard questions until *assembled members of the press* openly shamed him and forced him to ask her to come clean. Reportedly she smiled pleasantly through the whole thing and remained as tightlipped as ever. Minnie lived to be about 85 years old and took all her secrets to her grave.

But what happened next in Minnie Taylor's life, after Hazel Drew began to be forgotten, forces us to take a pause. Did she go back to the Harrison house and spend the rest of her days cleaning rooms and doing laundry? No.

After taking a prolonged vacation to visit relatives in Pittsfield, Massachusetts, Minnie returned to Troy and...got married. Yes, this "spinster aunt," as the papers called her, who despite being pretty good-looking, who never had a prior interest in men, suddenly gave up working, and took a husband.

She married a man named Edward J. Filieau, a French Canadian who settled down in Troy. Filieau was about eight or nine years older than Minnie, and a widower. He had five children from his first marriage and no doubt Minnie's domestic expertise would be essential to his family prosperity. The couple got married in 1909.

Though he is listed on the 1910 census as a wage earner and records show he often worked as a carpenter, Filieau enjoyed a good degree of prosperity. He was — wait for it — a member of the Republican Party and active in local politics, being especially prominent in the Prohibitionist Movement. He eventually became the Tax Assessor for the town of North Greenbush, a low-tier spoilsman's job. By 1920 he owned a home free and clear in Troy as well as a business; Filieau had one of ten companies going in Troy at the time selling bottled spring water. Bottling and selling healthy, clean water was an ideal profession for an ardent Prohibitionist.

Mr. Filieau died in 1939. Minnie went on to live another fifteen years, passing in 1954. She managed to raise the Filieau brood without ever having to work another job. At the time of her passing, Minnie had an estate worth, in today's money, over $100,000 and was able to bequeath legacies to her two churches and to eight nieces. The bulk of the estate was left to a final niece, presumably a favorite that lived in Averill Park. Her name was Hazel. Hazel Schumann.

Whatever Minnie Taylor did between the closing of Hazel Drew's inquest and her marriage signified a radical departure from four decades of life up to that point. We cannot help but conclude that Hazel's death was the catalyst for Minnie deciding to make this change.

Minnie Taylor, thus fiercely protective of her privacy and that of her family, grew up to be a very good secret keeper. She was the perfect person to serve as a domestic in the homes of the Troy robber barons, where discretion was as valued as good cooking skills. When Hazel died, Minnie likely had a suspect in mind, having access to knowledge of Hazel's intimate relationships. She feared innocent friends might be implicated while knowing that if the killer turned out to be one of the local elites — as was the case with Billy Brown — ratting them out meant hell to pay. Minnie had borne witness to what the Machine had done to one of its own, Thomas Hislop, even with all his wealth and power. She had no interest in getting tangled in its cogs.

So, Minnie did what she always did. She clammed up, she

protected her family, took steps to erase any possibly compelling evidence, and stuck to her guns through the bitter end. O'Brien, himself a Machine man, likely either overtly knew what she was doing or suspected and played along. When everything was said and done, Minnie preserved her reputation as a good and discrete domestic and leveraged her connections to land in the household of Mr. Filieau. Yes, that is speculation. But it's speculation that fits, especially as we continue to expose the clues that inexorably cause us to believe that there are facts of Hazel's murder that lead to a cover-up.

Ms. Mina
Chapter 9

We know very little about the full extent of Hazel Drew's friendships and relationships, largely at the expense of Minnie Taylor's obfuscation. Of Hazel's known friends, among the oldest and dearest was Mina Jones, wife of Frank Jones, and a former resident of Troy whom Hazel had leveraged her source of income to visit after she moved to Providence, Rhode Island. Other than Aunt Minnie it appears that Mina was the person in Hazel's life whom she knew best. Hazel was certainly Mina's closest confidant.

Based on what we know of Aunt Minnie's attempt to convince Mina to expunge her letters, she would have preferred if the existence of Mrs. Jones remained a secret. Nevertheless, Ms. Mina enters our tale of her own accord when she drafted a letter to the *Troy Evening Record* on July 13th. The letter was received by that paper on the evening of July 16th, and they made no effort to conceal its contents, instead choosing to run this piece of private correspondence as part of their daily news coverage of Hazel's murder.

WATERVILLE, ME, JULY 13, 1908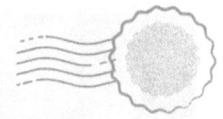

Troy Record—Please find enclosed five cents in
stamps, for which please send me papers that contain
news of the Hazel Drew murder. I am a former resident
of Troy and Miss Drew was a very dear friend of mine.
Will you please send me all the papers, if there are
more developments in the case, and I will forward
money for same.

THANKING YOU IN ADVANCE,
I REMAIN YOURS TRULY,
MRS. MINA JONES.

235 MAIN STREET, WATERVILLE, ME.

After the publication of this letter, all eyes turned to Mrs.
Jones whose relationship with Hazel Drew had to be probed for
a potential break in the case. Who was Mina and how was she
connected to Hazel Drew?

Mina Jones was born Mina Butler in December 1877 or
1878 in Waterville, Maine. Her mother, Jennie, was a native of
Maine and her father Peter was Canadian-born, though he
served in the 12th Maine Regiment of the Union Army during
the Civil War. Like the Drew clan, the Butlers were working
class, though educated. On the 1900 census, Mina indicated she
could read and write, as her letters demonstrate.

Mina Butler married Frank C. Jones in 1897, a man two
years her senior and also a Waterville native. In 1900 they were
living on High Street in Waterville in a rented house along with a
seventeen-year-old niece. At some point between 1900 and 1910,
the Joneses moved out of Waterville and spent some years living

around New York State, Massachusetts, and Rhode Island. Their son Charles L. Jones was born in 1905.

It is difficult to reconstruct when exactly the Joneses lived in Troy. Their son, who was five in 1910, was born in Massachusetts. By April 1908 Mina was living in Providence, Rhode Island, possibly without Frank. Adding to this confusion, the Joneses told the *Troy Northern Budget* they had known Hazel Drew for *thirteen years.* We have to believe this may have been a misprint or something misheard. However, if that were truly the case, they would have first met Hazel about 1895, when Hazel herself was a child. This would have been about the time the Joneses got married so it seems likely that Frank and Mina met Hazel through family. Minnie Taylor had an extensive network of relations, many distant, with whom she maintained friendships. Possibly Hazel attended the Joneses wedding, which would have been early in or even at the start of their relationship.

Following Mina's letter to the paper requesting more information about Hazel's death, the local authorities and the press got interested in her. As such the information provided by Mina regarding the case is scattered throughout various newspaper reports and is often inconsistent. She also wrote a letter to D.A. O'Brien, the only thing from which was disclosed is that Hazel had visited her in April 1908 when she was living in Providence, Rhode Island.

We learn a handful of interesting things from these exchanges with Mina Jones:

```
1. Their relationship was intimate enough
that Minnie Taylor was concerned about what
was contained in their correspondence, to
the point that Minnie asked that those mate-
rials be destroyed.
```

```
2. Hazel was twice assaulted in Troy on the
street, but in both cases, she was safe and
able to "beat off" her attacker.
```

3. Hazel had an Italian or Armenian stalker who had troubled her, even once appearing at the home of her employer.

4. It was with Mina that Hazel Drew visited Boston on her trip in April 1908. Frank informed the local Providence papers of this, though the story was apparently not picked up in Troy.

5. Hazel had a male friend who was either a boyfriend, suitor, or interested acquaintance, who was employed in a dentist's office in Troy. Mina could not remember this person's name. They met at a church Christmas party in 1906 and Hazel informed Mina that she had rebuffed a marriage proposal from him.

6. The issue of "the dentist" introduces a lot of confusion into
the case and it appears to have confused the investigators and newspapermen of the time. Hazel herself had dental work done, though when asked Mrs. Cary could not remember this dentist's name. Though Hazel had requested to go see him one night "after supper." Mrs. Cary did not believe a dentist's office would be open so late and denied the request. We are led to speculate that this may have been a cover to meet her friend.

It appears that Mina—or Frank and Mina together—told the press and the police that Hazel had a potential suitor whom she could marry at any time, who worked in a dentist's office. The press began to report that Hazel's suitor *was* a dentist and even a *young* dentist. In further confusion, the press began searching for Hazel's personal dentist under the assumption that he might be the same dentist who had a romantic interest in Hazel.

Hazel did have a dentist named Dr. Edward J. Knauff. His residence and business were located at 49 Third Street in the heart of Troy. After the police and press tracked him down, he revealed that he did know Hazel and that she and a friend had come to his address a few weeks back requesting an evening appointment. Dr. Knauff made it clear he did not do evening work and that they should return during normal business hours.

The author Ron Hughes speculates that it was in fact William Knauff, the dentist's son, with whom Hazel was acquainted and the request for an evening appointment was a cover to see the young man.[1] Hazel and William would have been about the same age, so this is not outside the realm of possibility. Dr. Knauff, 49 years old at the time, was asked if he was having an affair with Hazel Drew and he responded, "as far as I know I'm a married man." No one ever asked publicly about her relationship with other members of the dentist's household or business.

Mina claimed she did not know this dentist's office employee's name. Nor did anyone else know about this potential relationship. There were a lot of dentists' offices in Troy in 1908, so the potential pool of suspects is large. Also, since it is likely the person wasn't a dentist himself, that makes the pool even larger. There is also the possibility that this story wasn't true at all, and that Hazel Drew merely told people about this beau at the dentist's office to make them stop asking questions. We will explore her romantic relationships later. While the press found the line of enquiry related to the dentist enticing, in the end nothing came of it. Though we will give serious consideration to this person as a suspect.

Speaking of suspects, that brings us to Frank C. Jones. Frank was a man who lived with a lot of demons it seems. While living in Troy, Mina Jones worked as a dressmaker. We don't know if she did that kind of work in the other places where the couple lived, but we can assume so. It was good work that could be done at home with a small boy.

April of 1908 found Mina living in Providence, Rhode Island, where Hazel visited her and where she seemed to have been happy. According to Frank Jones, Hazel and Mina visited Boston while Hazel was in town. Providence, despite how far north it is, has a mild climate and hot summers, not so easily found in Maine. However, *something* happened to the Joneses that made Frank move his family back to their hometown of Waterville shortly after Hazel's departure. It is clear from her correspondence to Hazel that Mina was not happy there. And, in addition, Frank was not living with her.

Frank was living in Troy at the time Hazel was killed. He was working at the Fuller & Warren Company. Fuller & Warren were stove makers. As various census records indicate, this kind of foundry work was Frank Jones's primary career. While working there, Frank boarded at the home of the daughter of the factory's deceased owner, Martha Fuller. He was said to spend his evenings passing the time reading books.

Frank claimed he never checked in on Hazel during this time. However, Mina herself implored Hazel to check in on Frank. Mina wrote to Hazel on June 16, 1908, asking that she remind Frank that he had a wife in Waterville. This alone was enough for investigators to get curious about Frank Jones and his whereabouts when Hazel was killed. Frank was nowhere to be found in Troy following Hazel's death and had made his way back to Waterville and his family.

Frank told the police that he just so happened to leave Troy on July 3rd to visit friends in Boston. Apparently, this also included abruptly quitting his job and moving back in with his wife and son in Maine. Frank was eventually able to account for his whereabouts the day Hazel was killed, July 7th, and the police accepted his alibi. But the coincidence of his departure coinciding with Hazel's last weekend is suspect. We will have to deal with Frank Jones later.

The nature of Hazel and Mina's relationship remains uncertain. Hazel's brother Joseph told the newspapermen and investigators that Hazel had very little interest in men and preferred the company of other women. While her parents insisted she had suitors, her brother downplayed these claims. Were Hazel and Mina lovers? Mina expressed strong affection for Hazel in letters to Aunt Minnie, including using the word "love." But this, of course, may have been platonic.

We do know that Frank Jones moved his wife back to their hometown in Maine shortly after Hazel's visit to see Mina. She was clearly unhappy there. Frank himself persisted in living and working in Troy—where no doubt his wife would have been much happier. Yet he insisted on keeping her at a distance. They both lived the rest of their lives in Waterville.

Maybe it wasn't Hazel. As we go deeper into speculation, perhaps Minnie and Mina were lovers. Perhaps this is the reason she was so interested in having those letters destroyed. Everyone assumed it was to hide a trail leading to a potential man-friend. Perhaps not—perhaps Minnie was attempting to hide her own indiscretion, something Frank Jones had found out about.

Whatever it was Minnie wanted Mina to hide, it seems like it may not have had much to do with Hazel Drew. Mina cooperated with the police. She answered the reporters' questions. She volunteered to give information to the District Attorney. She also pushed back on Minnie and kept some of the treasured heirlooms from her murdered friend. This implies, too, that Mina Jones knew what Minnie was worried the authorities could find out and refrained from exposing it. Mina did admit that some of her Hazel materials were destroyed during the move from Providence to Waterville. Maybe that's true, maybe not. Hell, maybe Frank destroyed them in a fit of jealousy. We simply do not know. Further speculation becomes dangerous.

Mrs. Cary said Hazel told her a law student named Wolf had proposed marriage. John Drew said she had a fellow, but he cut her out at the time of her illness in early 1908. Mrs. Cary never saw any of these men at her house. The few men who spoke about their time with Hazel presented her as a girl almost painfully chaste—ice skating and taking them on endless trips to church.

Hazel Drew's parents' house in Troy, as it appears today.
Photo by the author.

Maybe Joseph Drew, who seems to have known his sister very well, was just being honest. Hazel Drew preferred being around women, whether sexually or otherwise. One of her favorite women was Mina Jones, whom she had just visited in April and who she kept a running correspondence with.

If indeed Mina had known Hazel for thirteen of her twenty years and been sufficiently in her confidence that Aunt Minnie feared the contents of her letters, then Mina should have suspected who her killer was. While we must consider that perhaps Mina's husband did it, it seems the police didn't take that possibility seriously. Mina was in the dark. Thus, it seems likely that Hazel's killer was someone who had come into her life recently and was the type of person about whom she was truly not at liberty to discuss. If Hazel and the killer had an illicit relationship, Hazel kept her mouth shut. Mina Jones had no suspects. If Aunt Minnie suspected someone (I think she did), she remained as tight-lipped as Hazel.

Frank and Mina Jones did not enjoy happy lives following the death of Hazel Drew. Mina died only a handful of years later, on April 25, 1913. Her cause of death was bronchitis and mitral regurgitation, a chronic heart disease. After filling out the death certificate someone wrote "acute" in front of bronchitis. Mina was dead at age 35.

Frank was gone only two years later, on February 17, 1915. Frank Jones died of morphine poisoning. His death certificate states that he was dependent on the drug and so the examiner "presumed suicide." I am not sure why suicide was presumed, as overdose from addictive drugs was a major cause of death then as now. Perhaps there were other clues we are not privy to.

For those who want to paint Frank as Hazel's killer—this is a powerful potential piece of circumstantial evidence. A man kills his young lover (or his wife's lover), has a guilty conscience, loses his wife, and slowly spirals downward, finally doing himself in. It is also likely that Frank, like a lot of people with laborious jobs, turned to morphine as a pain killer and eventually his dependency got out of control, and he overdosed. It's also possible the loneliness of life without Mina was just too much for him. Here was a man who just lost his wife a few years earlier—a wife who, by her own admission, was unhappy. Frank's failures as a husband were bandied about in the national press for that hot month in 1908. It was probably humiliating. Whatever led Frank to take too much of the drug on which he had become dependent, it need not be guilt over murder. There was plenty of depression in the man's unhappy life.

[1] Hughes, Ron. *Who Killed Hazel Drew?: Unraveling the Clues to the Tragic Murder of a Pretty Servant Girl*. Pennsauken, NJ, BookBaby, 2017.

PICTURES AND CORRESPONDENCES
CHAPTER 10

W hen Hazel Drew's trunk was found by the authorities at her parents' house it was full of letters, postcards, and a few photographs. A box of torn-up material, similar in nature, was also found in the basement of the Cary home, the site of her last employment. District Attorney Jarvis O'Brien had this material in his possession, much of which had been signed only with nicknames to disguise the correspondent. Hazel was a prolific letter writer and sender of postcards. She maintained friendships at a distance through this practice.

O'Brien worked hard to keep this material out of the press lest it embarrass an innocent person. This is, perhaps, a lesson he learned from the Billy Brown investigation in which her correspondence was published widely and fueled the salacious nature of the case. Presumably, all of Hazel's material was either purged by the police or destroyed in the fire that destroyed many Rensselaer County records years later. Whatever happened to those documents, they are lost. So, our ability to reconstruct Hazel's correspondence and the relationships she had through it is highly limited to what little hints were provided in the press. Mining the press for clues to Hazel's friends via her letters is greatly complicated due to the meddling incompetence and outright lies of one man: William Montgomery Clemens.

Will Clemens, to put it bluntly, was a liar.

HAZEL DREW'S BAG
FOUND AT STATION

Was in Suit Case, but Neither
Contained Any Clue to
Troy Murder.

CHECKED IN PACKAGE ROOM

District Attorney Not Satisfied with
Contradictory Statements Made by
Frank Smith, Who Saw Her on Road.

*New York Times, July 16, 1908. Everyone following the
mystery thought the discovery of Hazel's luggage would break
the case.*

This is not a libelous accusation. He claimed for his entire
life he was the nephew of the greater man to bear his surname,
Samuel Langhorne Clemens, better known as Mark Twain. Will
Clemens even went so far as to self-publish a biography of
Clemens in 1898, which critics accused him of plagiarizing from
shorter works by other authors. Will Clemens's obituary credits
him as Twain's nephew. But this simply was not true. According
to one of Twain's modern biographers, Mark Twain himself
referred to William M. Clemens as "a tapeworm."

In 1908 Will Clemens was working as a "journalist" for the
New York World, the tabloid paper run by Joseph Pulitzer.
Clemens was billed by his paper as the world's foremost criminologist. Clemens had no training or experience in this field,
even by the unchecked standards of the day. Rather, the primary
labor of his life was as a genealogist. He wrote several biographies
and genealogies, the most famous of which was on the subject of
Mary Baker Eddy, the founder of Christian Science. Clemens
also wrote bad poetry, novels, and something akin to an after-
dinner joke book.

Clemens liked to write about the deaths of pretty girls,
always introducing some grandiose mystery man into the mix as

the murderer. As such, he got himself to Troy soon after Hazel's body was found, no doubt sensing the similarities between her death and that of Billy Brown. Sporting fancy suits and even fancier business cards embossed with the *nom de guerre* of Criminologist, the self-appointed Sherlock Holmes of America arrived in Collar City. He went to work immediately making a mess of the Hazel Drew case, and in the process created out of whole cloth the Legend built on the supposition that Hazel was a sinning coquet and the kind of gal who needed to sneak away to Taborton Mountain to recover from an abortion.

Clemens's work circulated widely, and other papers picked it up, often without attribution. Thus, we are left with a situation today where we are forced to pick apart that which was written by Clemens and has no corroborating evidence and that which we can confirm as fact. A couple of key pieces of evidence upon which modern researchers rely are exclusive to Clemens alone and are quite possibly wholly untrue.

According to Mrs. Mary Cary, Hazel Drew left the Carys' employment on Whitman Court early in the morning of July 6th, the Monday following Independence Day weekend. Mrs. Cary stated that she asked Hazel if she would like to do some laundry, and the girl refused, instead stating that she was leaving. She then packed her trunk and a smaller travel bag and abruptly left the Carys' home. Before departing Mrs. Cary paid Hazel $4.50 in wages.

Hazel then walked to Pawling Avenue, according to testimony from Aunt Minnie, arriving at about 10:00am. She had a conversation with Minnie and stated that she was planning to go to Watervliet, a town directly across the Hudson from Troy, to visit friends. After Hazel departed from the Harrison house, she was never seen alive by her aunt again.

It is likely this story about going to Watervliet was either a lie on Hazel's part or a fabrication by Minnie. The police later interviewed Hazel's friends in that town—a Mrs. Moran and a Mrs. Rowe—and both reported they had not seen Hazel Drew in "more than a month." At 1:15pm on July 6th, a girl Matching Hazel Drew's description arrived at the Westcott Express

Company and placed an order to have a trunk collected from the Cary residence and delivered to the John Drew residence, Hazel's parents, at 400 Fourth Street in Troy. The trunk was delivered later that afternoon and Hazel's mother paid the charges for the delivery.

After Hazel's trunk arrived at her parents' house, she never accessed it again. Its contents were made available to the local authorities by Hazel's parents almost immediately after her body was identified. In the meantime, it apparently sat unopened in the Drew residence as her parents wondered where she'd gotten off to.

When the police opened the trunk, it was loaded with clues. Exciting, no? Hazel was a letter writer and she seemed to have a lot of sentimentality, so she hung onto things. Inside the trunk were a few keepsakes that tied Hazel to a wide range of individuals, all of whom had the potential to be her killer. The police thought this trunk would lead rapidly to a solution.

It did not.

The artifacts contained within, one by one, were dismissed by the investigators as they ran the leads to the ground. Throughout the investigation, and despite having the press constantly in tow, O'Brien and his men made it clear that they planned to keep the names of innocent people with a connection to the case out of the papers. The local Troy press, even the Republican-leaning rags, found this tactic frustrating. They complained bitterly right on the front page.

However, on July 14, 1908, the evening edition of *The New York World* reported that over 100 letters had been found in Hazel Drew's trunk and were in the hands of D.A. O'Brien. Many of these were "souvenir cards"— postcards—and the story ran "not one of the hundred bears a man's full name." Presumptuous, then, to assume they were all written by men, then?

The story then goes on to state that among these, six letters and cards, sent from New York and Boston, were signed only with the initials C.E.S. The paper reported that O'Brien was putting particular stock in these letters as potential clues.

"A mysterious writer, "C.E.S.," speaks of loving Miss Drew, and chides her for broken promises. Another blames her for "being a flirt"...The writer evidently cared a great deal for the flaxen-haired girl. Mr. O'Brien attaches particular attention to the "C.E.S." epistles, for he says it is indicated plainly in one, whose contents he will not reveal, that Miss Drew met this mysterious "C.E.S." in New York no later than June 15."

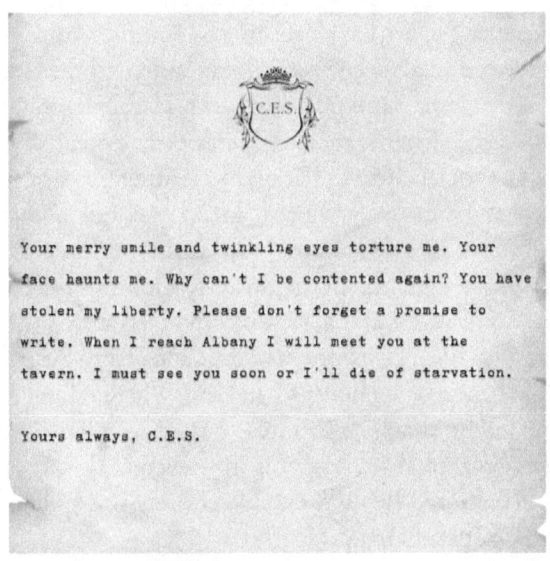

Your merry smile and twinkling eyes torture me. Your face haunts me. Why can't I be contented again? You have stolen my liberty. Please don't forget a promise to write. When I reach Albany I will meet you at the tavern. I must see you soon or I'll die of starvation.

Yours always, C.E.S.

This clue is so deeply tantalizing that Ron Hughes, author of *Who Killed Hazel Drew?* (2017), fingers C.E.S. as the killer.

The *New York World* was William Clemens's paper. The Troy papers did not run with this story. Remember, the reporters working this case were wandering around in a gaggle— they all got the same information at about the same time from the investigators. In reading the local Troy press it's hard to tell which story came from which paper, they're all written so closely alike. Yet *only* Clemens and the *World* carried the C.E.S. story with the letter transcript.

Interestingly, a couple of national papers that *do* mention C.E.S., describe the signer not as C.E.S. with initials, but as "Ces." Ces was a common nickname at the time for Cecil or

Cecily. This brings into question not so much whether these letters existed, but whether or not Clemens actually got his hands on them.

The local papers, rather than focusing on the "C.E.S/Ces" clue, on July 20th, carried the story of another letter writer identified only by initials, "W.C.H." Unlike C.E.S., we know who W.C.H. was because he was so upset at Hazel's death, he spoke out. His name was William C. Hogardt and he lived in Dedham, Massachusetts. He'd met Hazel in the summer of 1907 while they both vacationed in Poestenkill. He lamented the fact that he had exchanged letters and postcards with Hazel regularly until "a few weeks ago" when the letters stopped, evidence of Hazel shrinking her social circle in the period leading up to her death.

We know from other sources Hazel was not in New York City in June 1908. We know this from multiple witnesses, including Hazel's friend, Carrie Weaver, who traveled to the city with her for Memorial Day (formerly Decoration Day), the previous May. With corroborating evidence from Aunt Minnie and Mina Jones, we know when and where Hazel traveled. Again, no other source attributes these assertions to O'Brien. O'Brien never brought any of this up—even at the inquest. The Troy Papers ignored this C.E.S. clue entirely but spilled a lot of ink regarding friend Hogardt.

It was clear to the reporters who actually had access to the D.A. and his team that Clemens was just making things up. Some of the best, if sporadic coverage of the Hazel Drew case came from the Providence, Rhode Island *Evening Tribune*, which seems to have sent a reporter to Troy. This reporter clearly had not only unprecedented access to the investigation, based on his reporting, he also knew what he was looking at. He was present, as we will discuss, when Hazel's trunk was opened and provided the greatest detail of what it contained.

Regarding the letters in Hazel's trunk, on July 16th the *Evening Tribune* stated that "they cover a period of two or three years and most of them are written by juveniles. A few were written by adults and bear the postmarks of Boston, Providence, and New York...Mr. O'Brien states that in none of the letters thus far examined are there any love messages or other tokens that would establish that Hazel had a lover."

What emerges is a collection of letters preserved by a young girl and her "juvenile" friends. Hazel had just turned twenty and she'd been living and working in Troy since she was fourteen years old. Essentially, she had her trunk stuffed full of letters from other young people. But what about those letters written by the adults from Providence, Boston, and New York? Could those be from lovers? As O'Brien stated, the answer is simply "no."

On July 16th, presumably when O'Brien had a press gaggle hanging around, examining Hazel's things and engaging in discourse, the D.A. explained that not only did Hazel's letters not contain romance, the letters received from those big cities, Providence, Boston, and New York, were *from doctors*. "Letters were found in the girl's trunk from physicians in the cities mentioned but the district attorney refuses to make known their contents."[1]

There you have it. Unlike the Legend of a trunk packed full of love notes it becomes clear that Hazel's collection of letters were from her childhood friends and from the doctors she had been visiting during her travels. This also brings into focus the purpose of these trips. While indeed she was visiting Mina Jones and friends in New York, she was also seeking medical advice.

Hazel Drew had just come out of a serious illness. In addition, she sought a prescription for glasses for "head trouble" in 1907. The doctors who performed her autopsy found no tumor or other irregularities in her body, so her illness must have been one not readily apparent via the post-mortem. We must also assume that when this information was released to the press, the men from Providence were paying attention whereas Clemens either wasn't listening, wasn't present, or didn't care. Regardless, this puts the lie to his C.E.S. letter and much of his writing. The "adult letters" in Hazel's trunk were from medical men, not lovers.

I sat at my keyboard for an hour deciding how to write my next words—the problem of C.E.S. has dogged my investigation since the start, not just because a fellow investigator has fingered this mystery man as the murderer, but because his "appearance" fits William Clemens's pattern of introducing made-up characters into the narrative. Having looked at all the evidence and hundreds of sources, I simply do not trust that the C.E.S. letter —published in the Pulitzer papers—is real. While I believe that there were letters in Hazel's trunk signed C.E.S. or Ces, I do not believe Will Clemens had sufficient access to these in order to provide a transcript. O'Brien said as much—he repeated that he would not release the letters for publication. But Clemens wasn't done with this kind of fantasizing. On July 20th, while the "real" press was trying to run Mr. Hogardt to the ground, Clemens ignored him and introduced us to another pseudonymous mystery man: "The Knight of the Napp Kin."

On Saturday, July 18th investigators went to the Cary residence on Whitman Court to consult with Mary Cary regarding Hazel's relationship with a dentist. By this stage of the investigation, the authorities were attempting to run down the clues provided by Mina Jones. Tracking down Hazel's dentist was a top priority.

While at the Cary house, a box full of additional letters, postcards, and possibly photographs was discovered. It appears to have been found in the basement, near the incinerator, awaiting destruction. These items were similar to those found in Hazel's trunk, though many were apparently torn. In their report on July 20th, *The Troy Record* gave credit to the police for discovering this treasure trove of clues, however, Will Clemens lied and eventually took credit for the discovery himself. He also claimed to have discovered a rag bag of Hazel's discarded clothing, though nothing about that was ever mentioned outside of his reporting.

It was from this box of material that Clemens introduced another mystery man, again totally unrepresented in any other.

Here are relevant excerpts from Clemens's story:

———

Letters Received by the Girl Murdered
at Teal's Pond Show that She was a Favorite
of Men

By William M. Clemens
The World's Expert in Criminology

Troy, N.Y., July 20 — Light is beginning to break in the Hazel Drew Case.
There would never have been such a
black wall of mystery in this case had
Hazel herself been less secretive and
more frank and honest with her friends
and relatives.

Hazel was a flirt. She was vain of
her beauty and clothes, and during the
last year she dropped, one by one, her
girl friends and the young boys of her
life and began making acquaintances of
the more worldly sort

New York Men Involved
In May when she went to New York, she
brought back the names of New York men
and she had male friends in Albany,
Schenectady, Cohoes, and other towns.

Her mother had said that she did not
have a beau, whereas she had many of
them.

Planned to Go Away
On Friday Morning, July 3, she
received a letter in a man's handwriting written in pencil and within an
hour were carrying articles of clothing
from her room to her trunk, which she
kept in the cellar of the house. It

would appear that an elopement might have been planned.

Expected Other Money

It is more than theory to assert that Hazel Drew was expecting to leave Troy with other money than the few dollars in her purse, and that she expected to replenish her wardrobe at a very early date, necessarily with money furnished by the person whom she expected to accompany her in flight.

As an instance of Hazel's flirtations and the sort of men she attracted by her honesty and personality I am going to break the sacredness of her life by publishing the following letter mailed from Albany.

To my lady of the blond hair:

I am taking the great liberty in addressing this letter to you, my lady, but considering what a pleasant time you afforded us I cannot help but express our deepest sympathy for the loss of your glasses.

It is very possible that a pretty girl like you has many admirers and you understandably have a preference among them. It seems strange to me that we should both take to you more than to your girl friends but somehow you seemed to belong to a higher sphere, and considerably more sensible, modern, and have more pleasing ways. If we sent postals we shall expect others in return. "If Knighthood were in Flower I should live only for and have fond

```
clinging memories of my lady of the
blond hair and be faithful unto death
under the names of your
```

**KNIGHT OF THE NAPP KIN AND YOUR ARTIST
FRIEND HARRY**

```
She, poor, rural, innocent, whose
beauty was a real danger, soon became
the moth before the flame, and fate had
marked her for the fire.[2]
```

This is the article, ran in the national press, that birthed the "Legend" of the life and death of Hazel Drew. Here Hazel is presented as a vain flirt, chasing men in the Big City and planning an illicit getaway. Clemens would go on to make false accusations against a former waiter turned train conductor, misinterpret evidence related to Hazel's cause of death, accuse Hazel of being pregnant, and even create a hunt for an alleged clue in the form of a "missing" bracelet belonging to Hazel that wasn't lost at all, but with Aunt Minnie. All of which were meaningless distractions and fictionalizations that confused the case and subsequent historians.

I do not believe the Knight of the Napp Kin letter is legitimate. The police and the serious press made no effort to run this "clue" to the ground, while at the same time they spent considerable effort chasing the non-Clemens leads. Additionally, the letter contains a fatal error that is undermined by the facts of the case. "Harry," the Knight, alludes to Hazel having lost her glasses. True, at the time Clemens ran this story the whereabouts of Hazel's glasses were largely unknown. It would not be revealed until the inquest ten days later that they were not lost but had been found by two reporters near Teal's Pond. These were not a fresh pair of glasses but were identified by Hazel's optometrist as being the original pair he ground for her. So, the letter is an obvious fabrication meant not only to support the theory Hazel was flirting with men, but to explain her missing spectacles. Will Clemens twisted the accounts of Hazel's friends and family, which presented her as a good girl, chaste but outgoing who loved traveling and spending time with her girl-friends, as a conniving scarlet woman, leading a dark and meddlesome high-risk life.

This is the moment where fact began to merge with fiction in the Hazel Drew case. I don't know to what extent Mark Frost and David Lynch were actually influenced by the real story of Hazel Drew, but I like to think Laura Palmer is a tribute to Hazel: a pretty blond, leading a mysterious double life, is found murdered, her body dumped into a pond. Ironically, however, the inspiration for Laura Palmer may only exist as the result of the sensationalism of Will Clemens.

———

Barring Will Clemens's distractions, legitimate clues did arise from the contents of Hazel's trunk and the box of discarded materials. Hazel had in her possession a newspaper clipping featuring a young man which read: "Edward Lavoie has departed for Chattanooga, Tenn., where he will remain for the winter." In Hazel's handwriting was written "Oct. 6, 1907."

Lavoie was a young soldier from Watervliet who grew up in Troy but was recently living in New York City. When he was located by investigators, Lavoie did not even know that Hazel was dead, stating he was a "not that serious of a friend" of the girl. However, Hazel Drew was friendly with the Lavoie family and was close with Lavoie's sister. Edward's sister told the press that Hazel had "expressed her fear of some mysterious person."[1] It's clear in the weeks leading up to Hazel's death that Hazel was uneasy, as evidenced by her closing off her social circle to the likes of Mr. Hogardt. It would be easy to dismiss Edward Lavoie as a suspect were it not for the rumors (Clemens again) of Hazel's pregnancy. For those who wish to believe Hazel was pregnant and went to her uncle's house to recover from an abortion, note that Lavoie's date of departure is highly suspect.

District Attorney O'Brien, after sorting through Hazel's materials, presented the press with the photograph of a young man, perhaps no more than 20 years old, which had been found in Hazel's trunk. This revelation created considerable excitement among the journos. The *Buffalo Enquirer* blasted out a headline which stated that the trunk contained a photograph of "The Slayer." Sadly, it did not.

The investigators tracked down the studio that took the picture and from there tracked down its subject. The young man's name was F.W. Schlaffin. He worked as a packer and resided at 608 Broadway in Albany, across the river from Troy. He told the authorities that he had met Hazel Drew three years previously while skating in Rensselaer Park. The duo hit it off and Schlaffin escorted Hazel home. From there she invited the young man to call on her. Which he did.

Schlaffin stated that he called on her often, and Hazel always invited him to attend church. Not only that, but she also seemed to only invite him to attend *her* church, the favorite Methodist church she had attended since arriving in Troy, which she was particularly loyal to. This throws a wrench into the salacious theory that Hazel was hiding her relationships with men. Her church was attended by her employers and her friends and family and while living with the Hislops, she boarded with its minister. Any date she took to church would be witnessed by her entire social circle. F.W. Schlaffin was no mysterious lover.

Schlaffin informed authorities that his relationship with Hazel had just trailed off after a time. Certainly, constant invites to church were no doubt the equivalent of a repeated cold shower to a red-blooded packer. Schlaffin could not remember giving Hazel Drew his photograph, but at that time distributing photos and visiting cards containing photos was a common practice. The police did not consider Schlaffin to be "The Slayer" and neither do I.

This brings us back to William C. Hogardt. In the summer of 1907, Hazel vacationed with the Bly family at Poestenkill and it was on this trip that Hazel met Hogardt. There was an additional photo found in Hazel's things that was apparently taken on that trip with names listed. None of these corresponded with the "Knight of the Napp Kin" and all of those identified eventually proved to be wholly innocent of Hazel's death. No one knew anything or had a deeper connection to the girl.

Hogardt was seventeen years old when the police tracked him down. It was an annual tradition for him to vacation in Poestenkill, staying with a relative named Feathers. The young man was employed by the B.F. Sturtevant Company, a venerable old firm still in business today. Hogardt seemed to be fond of Hazel and told the police and press that he was mourning her. Hazel sent him twelve postcards, which he kept. This included a January 8, 1908, card that referenced her illness, a card that featured the campus of RPI, and a card with her new address at the Carys'.

In a few of these missives, Hazel references never hearing from "Gordon." This person turned out to be Gordon Hull, a nineteen-year-old man living in East Poestenkill. In fact, one card among Hazel's things was from Gordon Hull. It is tempting to add Mr. Hull to the frame as East Poestenkill is tantalizingly close to Teal's Pond, but D.A. O'Brien found these suspects came to nothing.

Hogardt received his last postcard from Hazel on April 22nd, postmarked from Providence, Rhode Island. This would have been sent on the fateful trip to see Mina Jones. Mina, in fact, remembered Hazel mailing a card to Dedham, Massachusetts, but could not remember to whom it was sent. The only text on the card was the girl's initials: H.I.D. The young man had no idea why Hazel cut off their correspondence, but it was clear in those last few months she was drawing her circle smaller. In the end, that is possibly the greatest clue we have from Hazel Drew's correspondence.

[1] *Evening Star*, July 16, 1908.

[2] *News Democrat,* Providence, Rhode Island, July 16, 1908.

[3] *Thrice-A-Week World,* July 22, 1908.

A Goodtime Girl

Chapter 11

I t is clear that when Hazel Drew departed the Cary home on Monday, July 6th, she did not intend to go to her parents' house that night. She told Aunt Minnie she was planning to visit friends in Watervliet, though this was doubtless a lie on either Minnie or Hazel's part. We have few clues as to Hazel's movements that day. It's clear that when Hazel left the Cary residence, she already had some kind of plan in mind, even if she only managed to concoct it that morning.

Hazel sent her trunk to her parents' home in Troy but took a "dress suitcase" with her. It contained, according to Minnie Taylor, the things Hazel had taken with her on their weekend trip. This same case was stashed at Joseph Drew's house while Hazel and Minnie wandered around Troy on Independence Day. Hazel leaving the Carys' with this case makes it clear she intended to stay the night away from her parents' home, where her trunk would be located.

On July 6th and 7th a few witnesses saw Hazel roaming around town with this case. She was even seen at Union Station telling an acquaintance that she was planning a trip "down the river." However, when Hazel Drew's body was found floating in Teal's Pond, the case was not with her. The police and press theorized that the killer may have made off with it. However, as

witnesses who had been in Sliters Corners Tuesday night began
to come forward, we know Hazel made her walk up Taborton
Mountain with her hands empty. Where was her suitcase?

In addition to this missing suitcase Hazel also owned a pair
of handbags, one of which was made of "Russia leather."
Russian leather is not leather from Russia, but rather leather
made from a process invented in Russia that involved hand
rubbing birch oil into the hide to make a hard-wearing material.
Hazel owning this bag raised some eyebrows as such a handbag
would have been a little pricier than what a servant girl could be
expected to own, as was the case with many of Hazel's possessions. These bags were also not with Hazel when her body was
found.

The mystery of these missing bags was solved on the afternoon of July 14th when investigators located the dress suitcase
checked at the parcel room of the Union Station. The bag was
checked by the manager of the parcel room, the delightfully
named Adelbert Atwood, who found it on the bottom of a stack
of cases. The time stamp indicated it was checked at 1:49pm on
the afternoon of Tuesday, July 7th. Atwood could not recall the
look of the person who checked the bag, but he was certain it
was a woman. He would testify to this at the inquest.

The time this bag was checked establishes firmly where
Hazel was in the last hours before her death. This would likely
have been her last act in the city before departing for Averill
Park, allowing her ample time to make all the trolly connections
needed to get her there. This also makes it clear that wherever
Hazel was on the night of July 6th, she needed her bags and likely
had them with her.

The contents of her suitcase were the typical items one
would need in 1908 for a short getaway. It contained Hazel's
black "Russia" leather bag, lined with gold. It also included a
gold locket and chain, heart-shaped and set with brilliants, a
comb, a toothbrush (Hazel was really into good dental care), a
nightrobe trimmed with pink ribbon, a comb, a washcloth, a
handkerchief, and a kimono. Curiously when these items were
shown to Mrs. Cary to confirm that they were Hazel's, she stated

that the comb and washcloth actually belonged to her, Mrs. Cary, but that they had been in Hazel's room. This means that Hazel left the Carys' home with property that belonged to her employer, implying Hazel did not mind stealing or that she left the Cary house without making time to unpack from the trip.

The odd inconsistency of some of Mrs. Cary's things being in Hazel's case, however, was ignored by the pressmen as focus shifted to the kimono. The kimono was an exotic item to many of the newspapermen working the case as it is typically misspelled as "kimona" in the papers. No doubt this is how the word fell out of Upstater District Attorney O'Brien's mouth when he pronounced it. Several of the newspapermen were sufficiently in the dark about this article of clothing that they wrote it down phonetically.

To be sure, this was an odd item for a chaste servant girl to own in 1908. Of course, Will Clemens ran with the presence of this clothing item in Hazel's luggage to confirm his "Hazel the whore" narrative and, in keeping with the conventions of the day, a lot of the more serious journos seemed to agree.

The inclusion of the kimono in Hazel's weekend wardrobe —and again after departing the Carys' house—led the more salacious writers like Clemens to conclude that Hazel had not spent the weekend with a bunch of ladies, or at least she had not intended to. Once again, assuming that Hazel would not be the kind of girl who would want to look pleasing for other women. The press at the time made assumptions we don't have to make, so we need to observe that the presence of a kimono could imply an intimate liaison, but not necessarily with a man.

We know that Hazel Drew sought out the company of men and that the chief experience we have documented gives us some window into her character and motivations. To understand this, we need to introduce another character into this story, Miss Carrie Weaver, a native of Ohio. She worked as a servant girl in the home of Professor Cary's colleague, Professor Arthur M. Green. Carrie was a recent—and very fast—friend of Hazel's. The two girls clearly liked each other. It was Carrie who accompanied Hazel on the trip to New York City for Decoration Day

(Memorial Day) 1908. Hazel had been on her longer trip to NYC, Boston, and Providence only a few weeks prior to that, visiting Mina Jones. It is clear Hazel developed a real appetite for the bigger city.

Carrie Weaver enters the picture with the arrival of a post-card sent by her from New Carlisle, Ohio to the Drew home and received on the day of Hazel's funeral. Professor Green hailed from Springfield, Ohio and the Greens had engaged Carrie only about seven months earlier. They were friends of the Carys, living nearby on Hawthorne Street. It was through Mrs. Green and Mrs. Cary that Hazel was introduced to Carrie, as Carrie had no friends in Troy.

Carrie left for a vacation to Ohio the day that Hazel quit working for the Carys, the morning of July 6th. Hazel had promised to see her off at the station but did not appear. This implies that Hazel's plans had changed on very short notice such that rather than go see her friend depart, Hazel spent her time packing up to move out of the Cary home.

Carrie caught word of Hazel's death as soon as the story hit the national press. She mailed an excerpt from the papers to the Green family asking if the dead girl was, indeed, her friend. Carrie would eventually be summoned to testify at Hazel's inquest but did not arrive on time. In one of the oddest turns in the case, O'Brien made absolutely no effort to prolong the inquiry to include information derived from interviewing one of Hazel's closest associates in her last few months of life.

On their Memorial Day trip, Carrie Weaver and Hazel Drew traveled to New York City via boat rather than by train, a more comfortable way to go. They were late coming home on Sunday as they did not realize that day boats did not run on Sunday (or they lied so they could extend their trip) and came home via a night boat. Carrie Weaver claimed they met no men in the city and she stated that were they to have met men she would not have been interested in the trip. Rather, they spent the vacation at the theater and riding around in "in cars," which, she stated, they paid for themselves.

A couple of curious things happened on this trip. Firstly,

Hazel Drew had her pocketbook, containing $6.00, stolen and Carrie agreed to front the remaining expenses for their travels. In today's money, that is just shy of about $200 so losing that cash would have been a considerable blow. However, the revelation in the press that she had her bag stolen explains where Hazel Drew's other handbag had gotten off to. It was stolen in New York and at the time of her death Hazel was down to just one purse, the "Russia leather" bag.

Mrs. Green, Carrie's employer, arranged for the duo to board at the Young Woman's Christian Academy (YWCA) while in the city. Respectable hotels for single, unaccompanied women to stay in were rare in 1908 in the USA. Unless you were very rich or very poor, getting a room without a man to sign for it was hard. Ladies would have to stay at a flop or be heiresses to get a place to stay.

The YWCA had a facility for ladies called the Margaret Louisa Home for Protestant Women, which charged around $.60 a night and was located on East 16th Street. This is likely the spot where Mrs. Green had intended Carrie and Hazel to stay. However, they did not. Carrie reported that they opted to stay in "private accommodation." This means either another hotel or a boarding house—or with friends. Remember, Hazel had already traveled to New York City just a few weeks prior to the Memorial Day trip and she supposedly stayed with unknown friends then.

The rules for boarding at the YWCA were restrictive for a couple of gals on holiday, with early curfews and the like. If the ladies wanted to stay out late at the theater and maybe do a little taboo stuff like take a drink or smoke, the YWCA wouldn't work. It seems likely they pulled a "bait and switch" with Mrs. Green, promising to stay at the more uptight YWCA and then crashing with Hazel's friends when they got to the city.

It is from here that Hazel Drew's adventures in New York City get complicated. Found among the torn and discarded items in the Cary home was a man's name and address in New York: John E. Magner, 449 Lexington Avenue. This address today is some seriously high-end real estate a few steps from

Grand Central Terminal, which fits because in 1908 it was a boarding house used heavily by railroad men. Mr. Magner, it turns out, was a Pullman car conductor who worked the old line that ran between Montreal and New York City, with brief stops in cities along the way, including Troy and Albany.

Magner's route would take him from New York to Albany on the New York Central Line where he'd have a very brief layover before his car would be hitched to a Delaware and Hudson line engine to chug on up to Montreal. O'Brien and his men sensed that Magner's address found among Hazel's things was a big-time clue, so they dispatched immediately to question the man. He claimed not to know any Hazel Drew, but the presence of her address in his things stirred both the police and the reporters to keep digging. The investigators ran immediately to Aunt Minnie to try to get some information on the man, but she fell silent at first, giving nothing up. However, after some "sweating" by O'Brien she eventually confessed that Hazel had mentioned calling on a train conductor in New York City, but that the man dismissed her and the female friend that accompanied her because he did not have time to show them the town.

Carrie Weaver made it absolutely clear that she and Hazel never called on a man while in New York. One possibility is that the girl who visited Magner with Hazel Drew was Edward Lavoie's sister who seems to have lived in Troy but would have reason to visit family in New York City. This implies, then, that Hazel had looked up Mr. Magner while on an earlier trip to New York, not the one taken in May for Decoration Day.

With this we finally get a little window into how Hazel Drew played her game. She had come into the possession of this man's address, possibly with the tip that he was the kind of guy who liked to treat a lady, and she cold-called him with another friend in the hopes that he would show them around. According to the rules of hospitality at the time, this would include paying for dinner. In return, the man would get nothing more than a nice evening out with some pretty ladies. The inclusion of a second girl on the visit makes it clear that this was not meant to be an exchange for sex. A male-female trip around town would be tantamount to "a date." Whereas a man showing two ladies around would be seen merely as him escorting them on their tour and would be more appropriate, without any implication of a more intimate liaison.

We know that Hazel and Aunt Minnie got up to this kind of stuff — they were seen riding in cars around Averill Park with men. Minnie had been employed at a fine hotel and she moved within elite circles. She would have known the rules of this game and, regardless of her sexuality, and probably played it to gain access to some of the nicer things in life that illuded her in her station.

Carrie Weaver says as much. O'Brien had local investigators in Ohio take a statement from Carrie Weaver regarding Hazel:

> "Hazel was a remarkable girl," said Miss Weaver. "I never could manage to buy the fine hats and swell costumes she wore, although our wages were the same. I never quite understood how Hazel managed. Not only did she wear expensive clothes, but she had elaborate luncheons at fashionable restaurants, besides many trips out of town. From making what Hazel told me she must have had an awfully good time when she went away from home. She said she had dandy dinners and that she was always treated fine. I really don't believe that Hazel went with any men, for she never told me, still it was always puzzling to me."[1]

This implies not that Hazel was buying these things for herself, but that she was "treated" to her luncheons and provided with gifts. This would add to the need for secrecy demanded by Aunt Minnie—she simply did not want to embarrass her and Hazel's social circle. A social circle which, it seems, Carrie Weaver did not have access to. But how did Hazel come by this specific tip related to Mr. Magner in New York?

George Peterson of the Westcott Express Company and William A. Humphrey, that station's baggage master, ended up ratting out poor John Magner, telling authorities they'd seen a Pullman man who looked like him spending time with a girl during breaks at the Troy station. For a moment the cops thought they had their man, but it turns out this was not Hazel Drew, but a girl named Anna LaBelle, who worked at the lace counter at Frear's Department Store, a spot Hazel frequented.

The press and police descended on Miss LaBelle, who seems to have had a reputation in Troy for being a bit of a wild child. LaBelle claimed she didn't know Hazel Drew at first. Taking an interview from her family home at 190 Third Street, the same neighborhood as Hazel's parents, she eventually admitted to knowing Hazel merely as a customer. Eventually, after further pestering from the pressmen, Anna would admit that it was in fact she who had given Hazel Drew John Magner's address with an entreat to ask him to show her around town upon her visit. LaBelle defended Hazel's innocence and honor in the press, all the while claiming to not really know the girl.

Miss LaBelle would go on to tell the authorities that she had seen Hazel at the Union Station on the afternoon of July 7th, before her death. For someone who barely knew Hazel, Anna LaBelle was full of information. In one of Hazel's postcards to Hogardt she mentions a plan to visit Poestenkill with someone named "Bell." It seems likely that this Bell was Anna LaBelle and that, indeed, she and Hazel truly did know each other. Regardless this lead quickly played out as it became clear that Magner had his eyes only on Anna and not Troy's other happening blondes.

At this point, the investigation got away from D.A. O'Brien in a way that is truly astounding—and *Twin Peaks* worthy. Enter another suspect, Mr. Samuel LeRoy. LeRoy, like Magner, was a Pullman coachman who boarded in New York at the same address as Magner. The two men seemed to have a casual acquaintance. Following up on leads from the letters in Hazel's trunk, the investigators scoured the town for one of the anonymous letter writers who had formerly worked as a waiter in an Averill Park hotel. This landed the investigators on Mr. LeRoy, who had worked at hotels out that way, including the Mansion House, but who had been away from that job for a decade, having come to Troy to wait tables at the Union Station. LeRoy was married and had two teenage sons, though rumors dogged him that he liked the company of pretty ladies.

Through some trick of fate, Mr. LeRoy was able to get his position with the Pullman Company via the intervention of Congressman George N. Southwick. Being a Pullman conductor was a damn good job and highly coveted. It would have been a massive step up for a man who waited tables. Accusations of infidelity and murder could imperil everything Samuel LeRoy had worked hard for.

LeRoy was a Pullman conductor who also had a billet on Lexington Avenue. He lived around the corner from Hazel's brother Joseph in Troy. He was rumored to like pretty girls. He was also suspected of having written some of the anonymous letters in Hazel's trunk. Though Magner fizzled out as a lead, O'Brien wanted to get LeRoy under oath. He dragged him and his family to the Grand Jury Room in Troy on the morning of Saturday, July 25th, separating LeRoy from his wife Rose, and swore them both in. A court stenographer, Louis Lowenstein, got the whole set of interviews down in what is arguably the most intense attempt to corner a suspect during the entire investigation.

It all came to nothing. LeRoy had an iron-clad alibi, as confirmed by his wife, his whole family, and even a handful of neighbors. On Monday, July 6th LeRoy spent the day aboard his train, making the New York run. This kept him tied up from about 10:40am until 7:00pm, when he returned to Troy and his home.

On the Tuesday, July 7th, the day Hazel Drew was killed, Samuel and Rose told the authorities that Samuel had spent the entire day at home hanging out on the couch. Their youngest son Harold was sick, and the husband and wife decided to see if their neighbor, Mrs. Alice Coleman would like to play cards that night. The LeRoys sent their elder son Martin to Mrs. Coleman's house to enquire if she'd like to play, but she was unavailable as she was going to help a friend prepare for her wedding scheduled for Wednesday, July 8th. The wedding party confirmed this as well. Samuel LeRoy practically brought the whole neighborhood in to swear to his location at home chilling on the couch while Hazel Drew was getting murdered. Nevertheless, the salacious elements of the press thought they had their man and went on to finger LeRoy as the killer.

The press confused Magner and LeRoy, speaking only of a "Pullman man" who was suspected of the killing. One Syracuse paper even accused LeRoy of using Magner's name as an alias! *The Washington Times*, playing Sherlock Holmes in their own way, believed they'd cracked the case by arguing that writing on scraps of paper in Hazel's things was identical to a pencil used by LeRoy. LeRoy blew this off, stating he simply used an indelible pencil which he sharpened flat, a common practice.

Samuel LeRoy took none of this lying down and went directly after the *New York World*, Will Clemens's paper. LeRoy lawyered up, hiring the best available, George B. Wellington, another arch Republican Machine Man, former U.S. Attorney, and future New York State Senator. Though LeRoy was only a Pullman conductor, he seemed to have powerful friends, as evidenced by his connection to Congressman Southwick. LeRoy and Wellington slapped the Pulitzer paper with a $25,000 libel suit, eventually netting a $5,000 settlement. That's about $160,000 in today's money.

These episodes, confusing and distracting, get us no closer to Hazel's killer and only add more suspects to the drama. Will Clemens accused Hazel of living a "double life." To an extent, I believe that was true. Hazel appears to have been what they referred to in her day as a "good time girl." This was a young woman who, frankly, just liked to party, without a focus on other things. Hazel spent the money she made. She knew she did not need to save, because she could, as she herself stated, get married to a good prospect at any time. It appears that through contacts with women like her Aunt Minnie and Anna LaBelle, she met men who were willing to take her and her companions out on the town for what was probably just a lot of good food and drink and some innocent fun.

This lifestyle, however, doesn't go without its dangers. What about jealousy? What about one of these men falling in love, especially if Hazel wasn't terribly interested in male company? What about a man getting a little too drunk and a bit hot under the collar? All of this could create a recipe for murder. In all honesty, it probably did. After all, we still don't know who Hazel was intending to impress with that kimono.

[1] *Evening Star*, July 29, 1908.

ILLNESS
CHAPTER 12

T he illness that caused Hazel Drew to seek bedrest in the Winter of 1907-1908 has been the subject of the most errant speculation among investigators, past and present. Though, it should be pointed out, not the contemporary doctors who examined her body or D.A. O'Brien and his men. Will Clemens introduced the idea that Hazel may have been pregnant into the narrative. A pregnancy and an abortion give us a male lover and an easy-to-understand motivation for murder. After all, Billy Brown was pregnant when Chester Gillette tossed her into Big Moose Lake and that story was fresh on everyone's mind.

However, there has never been a real need for speculation over Hazel's illness, because we *know* what her condition was if we take the time to investigate the local Troy papers rather than rely solely on tabloid journalism. July 18th was a banner day in Troy, New York for reportage on the Drew case. The word had gotten out through the region, by this time, that Hazel was dead and murdered. Witnesses were coming forward and her family was talking.

On that day, the public learned from several sources that Hazel Drew was not in perfect health. She had ear and eye "trouble." Her eye trouble was bad enough that she had to wear glasses "nearly constantly." Hazel's eye trouble required a visit to an optometrist, Charles H. Limerick, and he fitted her with a special pair of "nose glasses" made from a prescription.

Hazel took her health seriously at a time when a lot of people simply did not. She carried a toothbrush, got dental work done, and sought treatment for her eye and ear trouble from a professional optometrist and even at the Troy hospital. The adult letters in her trunk were from medical men. Hazel didn't let problems with her health go unaddressed. It was on Christmas Day 1907 that the illness that would leave Hazel bedridden for much of the winter took hold. She became sufficiently ill that Aunt Minnie came to the Tupper house to assist her in her duties.

It's odd even by the standards of the day that Hazel had to work Christmas. My assumptions are that the Tuppers were truly rotten people, that Hazel managed to conceal her illness, including Minnie assisting her, or that the Tuppers were away from home and Hazel sought assistance without their knowledge. Adelaide Tupper was Canadian, and they seemed to visit her old home quite frequently. Regardless, the illness eventually became such that Hazel could not continue to work and she sought refuge at her Uncle Will's farm where she spent some weeks, into February 1908.

Uncle Will would eventually go on to claim that he never bothered her during that time and largely left her in the care of his niece-in-law. No one called on her, no one came to visit. All witnesses agreed on this point. Rather than fleeing to recover from a secret abortion, the desire to find a secluded place for respite, far away from the city and the children in her care, as well as her own family keeping distance from her, implies that Hazel was suffering from a communicable ailment.

We know what causes communicable diseases today, "germs;" bacteria and viruses. But in the winter of 1907-1908 the germ theory of disease was not yet the scientific consensus. It would be another twenty years before the advent of antibiotics. In 1908 New York was ground zero for the national health crisis of the day: typhoid. Typhoid fever is a bacterial infection caused by *Salmonella enterica typhi*. Its symptoms are fever, abdominal pain, dehydration, and in the latter stages, painful rashes, internal bleeding, and delirium. Many patients would succumb to it after a protracted illness. The method of transmission is contaminated food and beverages.

New York City was the home of the disease's most infamous asymptomatic carrier, Mary Mallon, better known as Typhoid Mary. Typhoid Mary was a domestic servant, just like Hazel Drew. Typhoid was in the news and Americans at large were scared—but especially New Yorkers. Typhoid was deadly and as a result people were acting paranoid. Typhoid Mary was eventually locked up for life.

All of this would have been on Hazel's mind when she woke up feeling sick on Christmas Day, 1907. Best-case scenario it was a cold that would pass, worst-case scenario it was typhoid, and she ran the risk of not only dying herself but of infecting the family she clearly cared a great deal for. That's why I believe she ran from the Tuppers and to Taborton Mountain—to ride out whatever it was she had come down with in safety and isolation. This was exactly what the public health officials were instructing potential sufferers to do.

All that said, we know what illness Hazel *actually* had. On July 18, 1908, it was generally reported in the papers that John Drew, while being interviewed at the Cary residence, stated that she had "the grip." During her illness she lost her job and, according to Mr. Drew, her boyfriend abandoned her and married another girl.

The grip is an out-of-fashion term for the flu; especially pernicious and epidemic flu. A general perusal of contemporary newspapers indicates the winter of 1907-1908, along with concern about typhoid, was also a terribly bad flu season. Considering that bad flu and typhoid in its early stages have similar symptoms, neither of which could really be alleviated by a physician, it makes sense for Hazel to have sought isolation and care.

We can dismiss the salacious belief that Hazel sought isolation on Taborton Mountain to recover from a forbidden abortion. As we learned at her inquest, the doctors who performed her autopsy were unanimous in their belief that she had never been pregnant. The doctors themselves closed off this potential avenue for fingering a suspect.

Rather than fleeing in shame to hide a pregnancy, when Hazel Drew got sick, she did *exactly what she was supposed to do.* She got herself away from the vulnerable, she self-isolated, and she let the illness run its course. It is no mystery that Uncle Will didn't look in on her. He needed to work on the farm and couldn't afford to get sick. It is no mystery that her invalid mother, who could not afford to get sick, did not visit. Everyone merely sat back and waited for the girl to recover. When she recovered, she put aside her former life with the Tuppers and started a new life on Whitman Court with Professor Cary and his family.

Two Curious Lies

Chapter 13

As we move toward beginning to hypothesize a killer in this case a particularly interesting inconsistency arises around the very last hours of Hazel's life, shortly before her final departure from the Cary residence. For some reason, two key witnesses in this case *lied* about a seemingly unimportant detail related to Hazel's last night in that home that O'Brien and his men and subsequent historical investigators either ignored or failed to notice. The tipoff to the lies is, predictably for Collar City, an article of clothing, a second shirtwaist.

The only truly verifiable facts regarding that Independence Day weekend, as confirmed by reliable witnesses, is that Hazel Drew presented herself at the home of Mrs. Mary Schumacher (wife of John Schumacher), her tailor at 64 13th Street in Troy on the evening of Friday July 3rd. She demanded the garment for a stated trip to Lake George and—to Mrs. Schumacher's surprise—was willing to wait for it until 11:00pm. Hazel arrived with new fabric from the Boston Store—a formerly quite popular American department store—which Hazel was known to frequent.

According to Carrie Weaver, Hazel began concocting the

trip to Lake George during their Decoration Day (Memorial Day) weekend getaway to New York. Her whole family knew about the plan, including her mother and Aunt Minnie. Mrs. Cary said she knew about the plan and was quite surprised to learn that Hazel went to Schenectady instead. Lake George remains a garden spot, with the flavor of a European alpine lake, nestled in the mountains overlooking the Hudson. It is the setting for much of the action in James Fenimore Cooper's *The Last of the Mohicans: A Narrative of 1757.*

In Hazel's day, the train would take riders right to the southern tip of the lake, where they could deboard and take in the sites on foot. In the summer of 1908 Lake George would have been much in the local news, as the Lake George Steamboat Company had just launched the steamer *Mohican II*, which provided pleasure cruises of the lake. (The *Mohican II* still sails and tourists may travel on it to the present day.)

Hazel must have been excited for this trip. Mrs. Schumacher's house was on the southern side of the RPI campus, so leaving there at 11:00pm she would not have been able to get into bed before midnight. The Lake George trip would require an early rise—so Hazel seemed not to mind getting very little sleep. Aunt Minnie claimed it was her fault the duo didn't make it, as she didn't want to deal with the crowds. Keep in mind that she and Hazel still visited crowded places, attending a downtown celebration and going to an amusement park.

That inconsistency aside, we know from testimony by Hazel's sister-in-law, Eva, that Hazel dropped her bag at her and Joseph's house on Saturday, claiming it again that evening. From there, we have a limited understanding of what happened next. According to reports from the investigators published in the press, Hazel and Minnie went to Schenectady on Saturday evening to stay at the house of Annie Wyman—along with another woman, Etta Baker.

It turns out there was no such person as Annie Wyman, as reported in most newspapers. This relative was in fact Mrs. Anna C. Weinmann, a stenographer who lived with her husband

and family at 4 Pearl Street in Schenectady, a decidedly working-class part of town. Along with the Weinmanns, was a boarder named Etta Becker (rather than Etta Baker), a girl of 20, same age as Hazel Drew. Anna Weinmann was a maternal cousin of Hazel Drew, as was Miss Becker, who was Anna's younger sister.

Mrs. Weinmann was 26 in 1908, with a husband twelve years her senior. The confusion of names in the press was not uncommon. William Weinmann was a German-born machinist who was employed by Thomas Edison's mighty General Electric Company, headquartered in Schenectady. As of the 1910 census, the Weinmanns had four children along with Miss Becker living under their roof on Pearl Street.

The investigators allegedly confirmed Aunt Minnie's story that they had spent the weekend with the Weinmanns but it appears Mrs. Weinmann was not made to testify at the inquest. The investigators stated that no men were present, so either Mr. Weinmann did not count or was not present. The holiday was presented as a girl's weekend.

The Weinmanns were not rich people, far from it. So it is evident that a fancy shirtwaist was not needed for a weekend at their home. Nor was the kimono. In fact, it's questionable whether these clothing items would have been appropriate for a weekend trip to Lake George between a niece and a maiden Aunt. Either way, the presence of so many clothes in Hazel's bag implies that when she walked out her door, she was planning a very different weekend than the one that transpired. Either that or Minnie and her cousins simply lied about what really happened.

The whereabouts of Hazel and Aunt Minnie are not confirmed by a fully independent witness until late in the evening on Sunday. Roy Beauchamp, a conductor for the United Traction Company, knew Hazel and Minnie and witnessed them depart his trolley car between 10:30pm and 11:00pm that night. He stated that Hazel got out of his car at Whitman Court and Minnie got off at Pawling Avenue. Beauchamp stated they were riding the Beman Park car, which would have connected to cars coming in from Schenectady. Here is where we get a curious lie.

Lake George, New York, as it appears today. Photo by the author.

Roy Beauchamp told his story about witnessing Hazel and Aunt Minnie depart his train separately as part of the inquest on July 23, 1908. However, Aunt Minnie told a very different story to the press a few days earlier on July 16. When Hazel's bag was found, Minnie stated that she knew the contents of the bag Hazel had checked at Union Station because it contained the same contents she had in the bag for the weekend trip, including the kimono. Minnie stated she shared this bag with Hazel and Hazel walked with her to the Harrison house on Sunday night, where Minnie saw its contents.

We know this is not true, because Beauchamp swore under oath that Hazel and Minnie went to their respective residences separately. Hazel went to the Cary house, not the Harrison house. While these residences are close by, it is impossible to make this mistake. Herein comes the curiosity about the article of clothing. Minnie reported that Hazel had a second shirtwaist that had gone missing, which she claimed to have seen in Hazel's dress suitcase, the one checked at Union Station. When that case was recovered, the second shirtwaist was not there. That article of clothing was ultimately found in Hazel's trunk, but in the interim the investigators hoped tracking it down might lead to the killer.

It is clear Aunt Minnie did *not* see inside Hazel's suitcase on Sunday night—just as trolley man Beauchamp's testimony confirms. Rather, she either saw inside that case earlier on the Schenectady trip or never at all. Hazel may have simply removed the garment from her case after departing from Minnie. That seems slightly less likely as Hazel appears not to have unpacked her case and merely walked out with it after quitting on Monday, in the same clothes she had with her over the weekend. It is also possible that Minnie had no idea what she was talking about at all, and that Hazel carried an entirely different wardrobe with her for the weekend, repacking on Monday before departing the Cary home.

For some reason, Minnie wanted to make two separate claims that turned out to be lies. First, that she knew the contents of Hazel's suitcase and secondly that she and Hazel were together before she went to Whitman Court. Why? What was she trying to cover up?

This brings us to the second curious lie regarding that night. Hazel arrived home late on Sunday, with Monday being a workday. However, Professor Cary initially stated in the press that she had arrived back at his house "at a good hour." At the time of the inquest, he claimed under oath that she arrived late, after he had gone to bed. The backtrack of his initial statement would have come after the authorities, through Mr. Beauchamp, had established Hazel's true arrival time. Why the lie?

We know very little about what happened to Hazel that Sunday, after her day out on July 4th. She may have been in Schenectady with a bunch of gal pals—or maybe she wasn't. Whatever the case, two seemingly unconnected individuals found the need to obfuscate when it came time to provide information about her actions after arriving back in Troy on Sunday night.

Taking that into consideration, it's hard to imagine that Hazel's death following the departure from the Cary home was coincidence. We must suppose that Hazel's departure from the

Cary house—clearly unplanned based on all witness testimony —was a spur of the moment decision. Likewise, we must suppose that Hazel Drew's murder came about as a direct result of that departure.

Two curious lies. Why, after the girl was found dead, did Professor Cary and Aunt Minnie feel the need to change the facts of Sunday night? Why, indeed.

THE SPECTACLE OF
THE SPECTACLES
CHAPTER 14

H azel Drew's death certificate states her death was: "evidently caused by a blow on occipital region causing extravasation of blood in dura mater."[1] She received a blow to the lower back of her head, which caused a blood clot that killed her. The doctors who performed Hazel's autopsy confirmed repeatedly that this blood clot was the cause of her death. She had no water in her lungs, so she did not drown; Hazel's body was tossed into Teal's Pond after her death.

But how did Hazel receive this blow to the head? Such an injury may come from a punch with a bare hand, from being clobbered with an object, or from a fall. Put down this book and hold up your left hand, arm bent at the elbow at ninety degrees, parallel to your head, fingers pointing toward the ceiling, with your head facing forward. Now drop your arm toward your head until your hand rests naturally at the back of your head. *That* is the spot where Hazel drew received the blow that killed her.

The press, and subsequent writers, have described Hazel as being struck a blow "over the head." It appears most people interpret this to mean the top of the head, not the back. The County Coroner, Morris H. Strope, provided limited clarification in his final ruling, himself determining that Hazel was "struck" with a blunt object. Strope issued his ruling after the inquest and, following, there was no further coverage of the case. Just at the time people had enough information in the public record to start asking real questions, the questioning came to an end.

Coroner Strope's ruling reads as follows, mirroring the death certificate:

State of New York, Rensselaer County.

Inquisition taken at Averill Park, N.Y., July 27, [1908] and continued at Court House in the city of Troy on July 30, 1908, before M. H. Strope, one of the Coroners of said county, on the body of Hazel Irene Drew, which was found in the pond of Conrad Teal in the town of Sand Lake July 11, 1908. From testimony taken on the above dates I find that the said Hazel Irene Drew came to her death from extravasation of blood in the dura mater caused by a blow on the head from some blunt instrument in some manner unknown.

Dated, Troy, N.Y., July 31, 1908.

M.H. STROPE

"Coroner."

While at the outset this ruling might seem perfectly reasonable, it is almost impossible to overstate how truly inadequate these findings are, not only considering basic investigatory techniques, but based on evidence that came forth during the inquest itself. Now that you know where Hazel received that blow to the head, try this experiment yourself: pretend you are going to hit someone on the head and see just how awkward it is to land a blow in the occipital region. The victim must be facing away from you, and you will have to swing at them like a baseball player taking a swing with a bat, using something roughly bat-shaped. Or the person must be bent over or lying flat on their face, which would have caused wounds to the front of the head as well.

When hitting something—anything—our natural inclination is to go at it like a hammer or axe swing. Axe murders, for instance, were common in the nineteenth and early twentieth centuries and the typical wound from such an attack was to the top of the head, the front of the head, and the face. Even a killer picking up a rock to clobber Hazel with, would have brought it down toward the top of her head.

The rocky banks of Teal's Pond as it appears today. Photo by a local resident, used with permission.

The blow Hazel received is more consistent with someone falling backwards and smacking their head against a solid object, rather than being struck a blow directly by an assailant. We know that Hazel was wearing a corset when she died—it had to be cut off her. She was also wearing dressy shoes, more appropriate for walking around the city than traversing the rocky area of Teal's

Pond after dark. Imagine, again, yourself falling backwards, for instance on a slick patch of black ice when your feet shoot out from under you. Your immediate inclination is to flex your torso forward to prevent yourself from hitting your head. I have avoided much head trauma with this exact reflex roaming around downtown Washington, DC in leather-soled business shoes in winter.

Hazel—in her tight corset—would not be able to take this evasive action. She would have fallen back rigidly, with her forward roll limited by her tight clothes. She would have fallen back like a stiff plank of wood, landing flat on her back. Ordinarily, she would have survived this without too much injury. But, in this instance, her head struck a rock. We know this from the clues presented at the inquest—clues which, for some reason, the doctors, the coroner, and the Distract Attorney simply ignored.

Dr. Elias B. Boyce was a Sand Lake local and the first medical man on the scene when Hazel's body was found. Early in the investigation, he claimed to have seen Hazel in town on the day of her death, but if that story were true it doesn't appear to have had an impact on the overall investigation. While Boyce agreed with his colleagues, Dr. Harry O. Fairweather and Dr. Elmer E. Reichard, that Hazel's cause of death was the blow to the head, he went down a rabbit hole by insisting that the girl might have been strangled.

Boyce is apparently the one who removed Hazel's clothes at the autopsy. He found a piece of pink corset string tied around her neck, deeply embedded in her skin. He argued that this was the result of strangulation by the killer. Of course, always looking for a salacious angle, William Clemens jumped on this clue and spread it far and wide in the Pulitzer press, before finally admitting that he was confounded.

On the other hand, the younger doctor from Troy, Fairweather, apparently more experienced with postmortem remains, recognized the string for what it was: a part of Hazel's garments that appeared to be "choking" her because the gases from decomposition had swelled the body, tightening the string.

Nevertheless, at the final inquisition, Boyce stuck with testimony that Hazel might have been strangled, as the other physicians dissented.

It was claimed by a couple, Henry and Charlotte Rollman, that they witnessed Hazel Drew on Taborton Road the night of her death and that she was seen picking and eating berries. However, berries were not found in her stomach when she died and what little food her body did contain makes it seem she had eaten her last meal much earlier in the day, before heading toward Sliters Corners. Hazel had no water in her lungs, which makes it clear she was not breathing when her body hit the pond. All the doctors agreed that Hazel was killed and tossed into the pond.

Hazel's hat and gloves were found neatly placed next to the pond, along a cow path that led down to the water. The doctors and authorities believed this had been done by the killer, though I see no reason Hazel might not have done this herself to get comfortable. She was seen walking on Taborton Road with her hat in hand; it was an extremely hot day.

Hazel's face and hands were badly decomposed. She sank to the bottom of the pond when tossed in, only for the gases from her decomposition to cause her to float a few days later. It was a full day from the time she was first noticed floating in the pond until she was retrieved from the water on July 11[th,] and she'd been rotting in the hot sun for much of that time.

The doctors were confident that Hazel was a "good girl"— that is according to their experience she had never had sex and was not sexually assaulted. The use of the phrase "good girl" comes up repeatedly in discussing Hazel Drew and it was used each time in this context. From her mother to her friends to the doctors, they wanted it understood that Hazel was "virginal." As argued earlier, the doctors themselves sought to put the abortion theory to rest. Dr. Fairweather testified at the inquest that an abortion and pregnancy were simply out of the question.

In 1908 the police had no concept of a "secure scene" and the papers reported that thousands of people trod over the area around the pond. Nevertheless, the investigators tried to find clues, much sullied by the traffic. The pond was even drained in the hunt for clues. At one point a stick everyone referred to as a "club" was found. Dr. Fairweather went on to state that he thought this was the murder weapon and Hazel had been lured to her death. However, this item was never entered into evidence and was quickly forgotten.

A handkerchief with the letter "P" on it was found near the pond. However, the investigators assumed it was left by a camper or one of the many necro-tourists who visited the site. Incidentally, the only person with a surname starting with P connected to this case is the Reverend George P. Perry of the First Baptist Church in Sand Lake, who participated in Hazel's funeral. The item was dismissed as a clue.

The scene was a mess. Forensic techniques were barely in infancy and there was certainly no possibility of DNA at that time—it would not even be discovered for another 45 years. However, there was one clue left behind the significance of which everyone seemed to ignore.

What's missing? Hazel's spectacles.

When Hazel's body was found, though her gloves and hat immediately turned up, her glasses were missing. Remember these were quite a special set of glasses, ground specifically for Hazel from a prescription by Charles H. Limerick. These glasses, often called "pince-nez," from the French meaning "to pinch the nose," were popular in Hazel's day as low-profile eyewear, especially for women who might not like to have the arms of their glasses interfering with their hair.

Nose glasses fell out of fashion, eventually, because they could quite easily fall off the face and become damaged. Most wearers affixed them to their clothes with a chain and would pop them onto their face when needed. However, as we learned, Hazel's head trouble was such that she needed to wear these spectacles "nearly constantly," so it is likely she didn't affix them to her clothes as the presence of a dangling chain or piece of ribbon hanging by her face would have been annoying in her work; easy for children to grab onto, easy to get tangled while doing chores.

Hazel's glasses were eventually found by two reporters wandering the crime scene, Louis H. Howe of the *Evening Telegram* and John Kelly of the *Evening World*. Both men testified at the inquest as to what they'd found. These glasses were apparently tested for fingerprints, but if anything came of that it was never reported. It's clear if the killer had organized Hazel's things, possibly to make her death look like a suicide, he missed her glasses in the dark, so they lay *in situ* where they were found.

The spot where those glasses were found is the key to understanding how Hazel Drew met her end. While a number of newspapers reported that Howe and Kelly found the spectacles, only one newspaper described with any degree of detail where they had been found, the *Troy Times*, July 30, 1908:

> The glasses were found on the bank of Teal's Pond after the body was found. Louis H. Howe, a reporter for The New York Evening Telegram, testified that, in company with another reporter, he found the eyeglasses *at the base of a stone* [italics mine] near the place where the body was found in Teal's Pond.

At the base of a stone.

The doctors who examined Hazel speculated throughout the case that Hazel may have fallen and struck her head, rather than being struck directly by an assailant. Initially, an accident was a potential theory, though the presence of her body in the water precluded that. Rather, it was decided, finally, that Hazel had been struck by a blunt object "wielded powerfully." However, it must not have been wielded too powerfully as the blow to the back of Hazel's head did not break bone. Furthermore, the doctors confirmed that there were no other significant injuries on Hazel's body to indicate an attack. There was no struggle, she did not fight off an assailant.

The presence of these pince-nez at the "base of a stone" makes it clear that the supposition that Hazel hit her head was correct. Indeed, the "murder weapon" was most likely the exact stone by which Howe and Kelly found Hazel's glasses. As stated earlier, were she falling backwards, the tightness of her corset would prevent her from taking evasive movements, preventing her from curling forward. Were she to land on the flat ground she might have been alright. However, as she fell backwards, her head collided with the stone, knocking her glasses loose, and causing the extravasation that killed her. The force of her body weight was enough to end her life, but not enough to fracture her skull, as would a blow from a club or a rock being wielded by a killer intent on doing harm.

The cause of Hazel's death changes everything. Rather than a killer stalking her to the pond or coming across her and accosting her, we now have a manslaughter rather than a capital murder. Likely, rather than being assaulted by a weapon, Hazel was shoved in a fit of anger, and her leather-soled shoes, the darkness, her corset, and the presence of that stone caused what should have been no more than a mild fall to lead to her death. There were no other signs of violence or struggle, so this single act of malice killed her. Likely her assailant panicked, tried to stage a makeshift suicide by tossing her into the water, couldn't find her glasses in the dark, and fled, counting on the fact she was a simple servant girl whose death would be ignored by authorities.

Hazel's killer didn't plan to become a murderer when he met her at Teal's Pond. They met, they argued, things got heated, he shoved her, she fell, hit her head, and died. The killer did not have his wits about him and panicked, though he was intelligent enough to understand what he needed to do to throw the immediate scent off his trail.

This was a man who took the coward's way out. He could probably play the whole thing off as an accident, had he been one of her boyfriends or a friendly acquaintance. He could simply race down to Crape's Hotel and beg for help, owning what he'd done. I don't believe the murderer came to Teal's Pond to kill, but when he did end her life, he faced the prospect of not just having to explain what happened to the police—he faced the threat of losing his *reputation* as a person of good standing, and the money and position that goes along with it. The happenstance of being out there alone with Hazel, not just the fact of her death, would have been enough to cost her killer *everything*.

Hazel's killer wasn't some charcoal burner or lovelorn working-class kid she'd met at the ice rink or the Methodist Church. No, the killer was the type of person who had no business in Hazel's company and the revelation of his presence out there on Coon Teal's property that night would be enough to end him. I think Jarvis O'Brien and his crew probably knew that. They, themselves, were men of position and power who knew the score. No doubt at least a couple of them had a wandering eye and took the occasional stroll with a gal they were supposed to leave alone. O'Brien was no fool. His handling of the case cost him his career in the D.A.'s office, so his failure to follow-up these very real clues meant only one thing: Hazel Drew's murderer was one of his own, one of Troy's Great and Good, and he had to be protected.

[1] The death certification is found on page 157 of register number 271, on file in the town of Sand Lake.

TWIN PEAKS VIBES

CHAPTER 15

W hen I began this investigation, I never had an expectation that any aspect of it would in any way be reminiscent of the *Twin Peaks* universe, beyond, the initial conceit that Hazel Drew was the inspiration for Laura Palmer. David Lynch took as his muse the land and quirky people of Washington State and the wider Pacific Northwest, where he grew up. However, it quickly became apparent that the native and colonial lore of Upstate New York, especially the ancient and sacred site of Saratoga Springs and the land centering Troy is, arguably, the closest thing one may ever find to a "real" *Twin Peaks*.

To understand why, we must have a deeper appreciation for what Americans were like over a century ago, in that time before the technological horrors of the two World Wars recalibrated our Western *zeitgeist* from one of religion and spirituality to science and objectivity. We like to think of modern Americans as mired in superstition, watching cable television ghost-hunting shows, slapping Bigfoot stickers on our SUVs, and pondering if long-ago alien visitors built the Pyramids. In fact, in 1908—and for most of the preceding century—superstition was the order of the day. Newspapers were replete with horoscopes and announcements of "spiritualist meetings," Mary Todd Lincoln, wife of the assassinated President was obsessed with contacting the "Other Side." Even the paragon of industrial science, Thomas Alva Edison, attempted to invent a "Spirit Phone" to contact the dead, technology he thought would eventually become commonplace.

During Hazel's age, the afterlife, for most people, was a certainty, not a question or a hope. It was a concrete place, be it Heaven or Hell or some other more nebulous thing, and many people like Edison himself thought it was just a matter of time before Humanity's rapidly advancing technology would tap a means of contacting it. Interestingly, the great era of Spiritualism, into which Hazel Drew was born, began about two hundred miles to the west of Troy, at a small cabin owned by John Fox, in 1848. The foundations of the site are still present.

Leah, Margaretta, and Catherine (Kate) Fox did not invent the séance and mediumship in general, but they certainly created their modern versions and are the "team" most closely associated with the emerging Spiritualist brand. The three sisters grew up in a small house not too far from Rochester in the hamlet of Hydesville that had a reputation for being haunted. Notably, the Foxes' parents frequently heard bumps and noises in the night, saw furniture move, and other alleged paranormal events.

Eventually, the girls developed a routine for being able to talk to these disembodied spirits. To make a long story short, as is wont with sensational tales, it was not long before the whole business got out of hand and the Fox sisters were making large money performing séances in New York City, following some early demonstrations in Rochester and the surrounds. Spiritualism was starting to take off and their methodology, which included pops, noises, table rapping, and moving objects, became the standard business model. At the time Hazel Drew died, spiritualism was big business.

On Tuesday, July 21st the Wilmington, Delaware *Evening Journal* concluded their daily coverage of the Hazel Drew story with an announcement that Hazel's mother, out of desperation, had turned to a "pscychic" [sic] with clairvoyant powers for assistance in solving the murder. This person, a mystic supposedly of local repute, stated: "give me time...That girl was brought here dead. She was killed down the road at a place where the bushes are thick and—." It was further reported this mystic had gone over the scene at Teal's Pond and, on that very Tuesday night, would be calling on the spirits to reveal clues about the case. Presumably one of these spirits would have been Hazel's ghost herself.

The paranormal lean to the case was not contained to the Drew family. Throughout the course of the investigation, District Attorney O'Brien dropped references to the newspapers about receiving letters from the citizenry regarding the case. However, he was often coy when describing the contents of these missives. On July 26th, the Troy *Northern Budget* noted that letters received by the D.A. during that week were written by people "dreaming of the murder." Even the cursory *Twin Peaks* fan will note that receipt of vital information in the form of dream knowledge is a major plot device in the series. It is eerily coincidental that, as the paper states, the clairvoyant citizens of Troy, through their dreams "suggested plans for the capture of the murderer."

The *Northern Budget*, like a lot of popular media of the era (and today, if we are honest), leaned heavily on the mystical angle of Hazel Drew's death. One of the last news stories to be carried about her ran in the *Northern Budget* on August 2nd, after the investigation had ended, and featured the downright comical (and truly disrespectful) pontifications of Brooklyn astrologer "Professor" William Maccabee. Through an "appeal to the occult," he determined that Hazel had died as the result of the influence of several "evil planets" at 9:18pm. Beyond that guess, his contribution to the case included little more than an extensive horoscope for Hazel; doubtless a commercial for his business enterprise.

Hazel herself, though clearly an extremely stalwart and pragmatic person, seemed not to be entirely immune from dabbling in the Spiritualist traditions of her day. As reported in the Troy *Times* on July 22nd, Hazel's close friend Mina Jones wrote to Hazel's Aunt Minnie Taylor on July 16th informing her that

Hazel had seen a fortune teller who "foretold that Hazel Drew would meet with a sudden death during this year..." According to Mina, Hazel laughed the incident off. Nevertheless, the case from the get-go had a paranormal aspect to it.

Of these "occult" occurrences the most dramatic came from Hazel's mother, Julia. As noted, she appears to have engaged a psychic to assist in ferreting out the killer, obviously to no avail. However, on July 28th no less of a source than the Grey Lady herself, the *New York Times* published a story with the provocative headline "Mother of Troy Girl Asserts She Was Hypnotized." Like other Spiritualist conceits of the era, hypnotism— also called Mesmerism—was a popular and faddish movement that centered around placing people in a trance to get them to perform acts or divulge information out of character for their waking state.

A number of papers picked the story up, including the *Washington Post*, clearly echoing whatever interview Mrs. Drew had given. The most detailed version of the story I was able to find came from the *Richmond Palladium and Sun Telegram*, published the day after the *Times* on July 29th. This story states that Mrs. Drew refuted the theory that her daughter committed suicide. She followed up by saying: "I am sure Hazel did not commit suicide...She was happy and had everything she wanted. If anything had been wrong she would have come to me. She always did, and I gave her everything she asked. I believe it was some one [sic] who was well to do, and who had Hazel in his control, who took her out to Averill Park. He hypnotized my Hazel and she did whatever he asked of her. He took her out there while she was under his influence and murdered her."

District Attorney O'Brien saw no value in this statement or its relevance as a clue. The Troy *Record* reported on July 29th as well that O'Brien stated the matter was "absurd." He went as far as to deny that whatever interview had led to the story—though reported across multiple outlets, including two national papers of record—had never even occurred. He affirmed that Mrs. Drew "is careful in all of her statements." In a way this rebuttal from the DA sounds a bit like a threat. More on that point later.

Mrs. Drew, like the Fox sisters themselves, was a Methodist. Their collective theology allowed for what my father, an old West Texas curmudgeon, would call some "big talking bullshit." Grieving people are desperate. Grieving people with unconventional beliefs will turn to those beliefs at times of desperation. We can expect a grieving mother who grew up in an environment steeped in spiritualism, to take mystics, fortune tellers, and murdering hypnotists seriously.

But surely, we don't have to take all that seriously, do we? At this point you, the reader, would be right to assume I am including this vignette as fan service for the *Twin Peaks* enthusiasts among you.

Except.

Except over the course of my investigation I have discovered absolute proof that my chief suspect—the person whom I believe killed Hazel Drew—was in fact involved in *hypnotism.*

Queue the *Twin Peaks* intro music.

PART THREE
JUSTICE

THE ROAD TO
TEAL'S POND
CHAPTER 16

Hazel Irene Drew's walk up Taborton Road to meet her destiny took place on July 7, 1908. She arrived at her destination at roughly sunset and the events from that point until her heart took its last beat, remain a mystery. Her walk that night was not a random matter of happenstance; it came as the result of a chain of events possibly months in the making. Understanding those events builds a timeline to help identify the people, locations, and circumstances that revolved around Hazel preceding and following her death.

Key to any such timeline in this case would be the crucial events of July 6—July 7, 1908, and the time period between Hazel's departure from the Cary house and her death at Teal's Pond. O'Brien would have had several advantages over the modern investigator. He was there live on the scene and could scout for witnesses, ask questions, and probe directly for clues. He also had the facts in hand and unlike the present researcher did not have to sift through reams of yellow journalism to sort reality from sensationalism. On the other hand, he did not have access to a computer with tools for sorting notes, doing keyword searches across hundreds of newspapers, and easily fact-checking a wide array of information via internet resources.

I have attempted to build my own timeline of the events relevant to Hazel Drew's murder. My own notes are much more detailed, but I have provided a summary here to assist the reader and, hopefully, subsequent researchers in drawing their own conclusions. Many of the events outlined in this case were revealed publicly at Hazel's inquest. However, for clarity, they are presented in the timeline at the dates and times at which they occurred, not when they were reported. Here, without flourish, are the key events related to the death of Hazel Drew.

After more than a century of being forgotten, Hazel's community is starting to remember. This marker was erected in 2024 near the site of the William Taylor farm, across the road from where Hazel perished at Teal's Pond.

HAZEL'S TIMELINE
CHAPTER 17

June 3, 1888

Hazel Irene Drew born to John and Julia(née Taylor) Drew at Poestenkill, Rensselaer County New York on or in the vicinity of Blue Factory Road.

Circa 1895

Hazel Drew met Frank and Mina Jones, beginning a thirteen-year friendship.

December 1906

According to Mina Jones, Hazel Drew met her anonymous friend who either was a dentist or worked in a dentist's office "two years ago last Christmas," fixing the date of this meeting in 1906. This may have been the time when Hazel had her notable dental work done.

February 8, 1907

Charles H. Limerick of 284 River Street sold Hazel Drew her pair of prescription "nose glasses."

Summer 1907

Hazel Drew stayed at the Bly residence with Gordon Hull and others. Hazel also spent a week with John Link. A sketch of Hazel made by an artist while she was staying with Link was found at the Cary residence.

December 1907 — January 1908

Hazel Drew was ill on Christmas Day, requiring assistance in her duties from her Aunt Minnie Taylor. On January 8, 1908 Hazel stated in a letter to William C. Hogardt that she was sick at New Years. Hazel left the Tupper house on January 9, and moved into the residence of her uncle William Taylor, under treatment for "the grip" by her sister-in-law Eva Drew. On January 23, John Tupper fired Hazel by mail, sending her a severance letter and some money.

February 1908

Hazel Drew began working for E.R. Cary and his wife Mary in "early February."

February 3, 1908

In a postcard to William C. Hogardt, Hazel Drew stated that she was taking a vacation and living at her parents' house, 400 4th Street, Troy.

February 15, 1908

Reports of William Taylor getting a shave at Blake's Hotel and that he was seen later with a youngish woman, fair complected with dark eyes in a wagon at Averill Park. Many assumed this woman was Hazel Drew, however by her account to William C. Hogardt, she was already living with her parents or would soon be at the Cary house. Additionally, Hazel Drew had blue eyes. William Taylor would claim the last time he saw Hazel was in early February, while she was staying with him during her illness.

March 7, 1908

In a postcard to William C. Hogardt, Hazel Drew stated that she liked her new home, the Carys on Whitman Court.

March 1908

In late March, Stella and Kate Karner of Troy visited the William Taylor farm. Many assumed that Hazel Drew was one of these two women, throwing suspicion on Taylor's claim he had not seen Hazel since early February. However, Eva Drew and Stella Karner testified at Hazel Drew's inquest that Stella and Kate Karner had visited the Taylor farm and that Hazel Drew was not with them. Stella Karner wore glasses like Hazel's and, thus, this may have been the source of the confusion.

April 1908

Early April, Joseph and Eva Drew stopped
working for William Taylor and left his
farm. Shortly thereafter Frank Richmond and
his wife went to work for Taylor, residing
at the farm.

April — May 1908

During late April through (possibly) early
May, Hazel Drew traveled to New York City,
Boston, Massachusetts, and Providence, Rhode
Island. While in New York, Hazel visited
with unknown friends, but she stayed with
Mina Jones during her time in Providence,
taking a short trip to Boston with Mina. In
New York City, Hazel and another unknown
woman, attempted to meet with Pullman Car
conductor John E. Magner, who boarded at 449
Lexington Avenue. However, Magner was
unavailable to show the women around town.
Hazel received Magner's address from Anna V.
LaBelle, who worked at the lace counter at
Frear's Department Store in Troy.

April 22, 1908

William C. Hogardt received his last postcard from Hazel Drew, postmarked Providence,
Rhode Island. At this time Hazel was
visiting Mina Jones.

May 1908

According to Dr. Edward J. Knauff, Hazel
Drew and another girl made an evening call
to his office in early May requesting dental
work be done. Knauff informed the women that

he did not work evenings and asked them to reschedule. The women stated they would try to return during the day, but they did not.

May 29-31, 1908

Hazel Drew and Carrie Weaver traveled to New York City for the Decoration Day (Memorial Day) weekend. They traveled by boat, with plans to stay at the Young Woman's Christian Academy (YWCA) as arranged by Mrs. Green, wife of Professor Arthur Green and Carrie Weaver's employer. According to Carrie, the girls opted to stay at a "private accommodation." Early in the trip Hazel lost her pocketbook containing $6.00, and Carrie paid Hazel's way for the remainder of the trip. According to Carrie Weaver they spent the weekend at the theater and "riding around in cars." On Sunday May 31, they miscalculated the Sunday boat schedule and returned home via the night boat, as the day boat was not available. It was on this trip that Hazel Drew first mentioned to Carrie Weaver her plans to visit Lake George over the upcoming July 4th holiday weekend.

June 12, 1908

Mina Jones wrote a letter to Hazel that she (Mina) was upset she (Mina) had moved from Providence, Rhode Island to Waterville, Maine. Mina's husband Frank Jones was working in Troy at that time and Mina asked Hazel to look him up and call attention to his family in Maine. It is not established if Hazel reached out to Frank Jones.

June 28, 1908

Miss Lilly Robertson witnessed Hazel Drew at Prospect Park in Troy. This was the Sunday before Hazel's last weekend.

July 2, 1908

Mrs. Julia Drew, Hazel Drew's mother, last saw Hazel alive. Reportedly, Hazel did not mention a desire to leave the Carys' employment during this visit. Mrs. Drew informed Hazel that her brother, Willy, was staying at the Sowalskie's farm, in the vicinity of Taborton. Mrs. Drew later informed authorities that Hazel had not visited the family very often recently nor had she spent time at her uncle William Taylor's farm since her illness. Hazel Drew borrowed $2.00 from her mother before her death, which must have occurred at this July 2nd meeting.

July 3, 1908

In the evening, Hazel Drew arrived at Mrs. Mary Schumacher's house at 64 13th Street in Troy, requesting that Mrs. Schumacher make her a shirtwaist. Hazel brought new fabric purchased from the Boston Store. Hazel settled her debts with Mrs. Schumacher, paying her $3.00, the modern equivalent being about $95.00. Hazel waited for the shirtwaist to be made, departing Mrs. Schumacher's house at about 11:00pm.

July 4 − 6, 1908

Frank Jones, Mina Jones' husband, allegedly spent this weekend in Boston.

July 4, 1908

Unknown time prior to departure from the Cary house: Mrs. Mary Cary paid Hazel Drew $4.50, the modern equivalent being about $148.00.

Morning: Hazel Drew left her dress suitcase at the house of her brother Joseph Drew, 1617 7th Avenue, Troy. Joseph did not see Hazel, as she only interacted with Eva Drew, his wife.

11:00am: John Drew, Hazel Drew's father, last saw Hazel alive, possibly at Franklin Square, Uptown Troy, on a trolley car.

Approximately 11:00am – approximately 5:00pm: According to Minnie Taylor she talked Hazel out of taking her trip to Lake George (Minnie did not wish to deal with crowded trains) and the duo went to see the Independence Day Parade in Troy and then went to Rensselaer Park, a popular Troy amusement park.

Approximately 4:00pm: A young woman witnessed Hazel Drew and another woman – most likely Minnie Taylor – on Fulton Street, Troy, likely on their way to Joseph Drew's house, nearby.

Approximately 5:00pm: Hazel Drew collected her dress suitcase from Joseph Drew's house, departing, for Schenectady. Hazel once again did not interact with her brother.

Evening: Hazel Drew and Minnie Taylor arrived at the home of Mrs. Anna C. Weinmann at 4 Pearl Street, Schenectady.

Evening, Sliters Corners: Conrad Teal heard noises from the vicinity of Teal's Pond. Adjacent to Teal's Pond, Lawrence Gruber was camping and was the possible source of these noises. Late that night Chris Crape saw a "mysterious car" pass his hotel, headed for Teal's Pond, also witnessing its return. Investigators would later determine this car was driven by Harold D. Neach.

July 5, 1908

Hazel Drew and Minnie Taylor allegedly spent Sunday at the home of Anna Weinmann in the company of relatives, at 4 Pearl Street, Schenectady. According to Minnie Taylor, Hazel and Minnie departed the Weinmann home at approximately 9:00pm. Roy Beauchamp, a conductor for the United Traction Company, who knew Hazel and Minnie, witnessed the women depart his trolley car between 10:30pm and 11:00pm. Beauchamp stated that Hazel got off his car at Whitman Court and Minnie got off at Pawling Avenue. Beauchamp stated they were riding the Beman Park car, which would have connected to cars coming in from Schenectady. Minnie Taylor, however, stated Hazel and she got off at the same stop and walked to the Harrison house, Minnie's employer. Minnie further stated that she and

Hazel shared the dress suitcase and that it was at the Harrison home where Minnie unpacked her clothes from Hazel's suitcase. However, Beauchamp's testimony at Hazel's inquest regarding their departure from his car contradicts this. Regarding Hazel's arrival time at the Cary home, Professor Cary provided contradictory statements, first claiming that Hazel arrived home "at a good hour" and later telling Hazel's inquest that Hazel arrived after he "retired."

Evening, Sliters Corners: Conrad Teal once again heard noises coming from Teal's Pond.

July 6, 1908

2:00am: Chris Crape claimed he heard a mysterious car pass his hotel around this time. However, investigators determined that he was mistaken (possibly influenced by the offer of a reward related to Hazel Drew's death) and this was, in fact, the car driven by Neach witnessed on the evening of July 4.

Morning, undetermined: Carrie Weaver departed by train for her vacation to Ohio. Hazel Drew had planned to see her off but failed to do so.

Morning, before 10:00am: According to Mary Cary, wife of Professor E.R. Cary and Hazel Drew's employer, Hazel was asked to "do some laundry" by Mrs. Cary. Hazel declined to do the laundry and, rather, went to her room, where she packed her trunk and dress suitcase and departed the Carys' employment. At

this time, Hazel Drew may have torn up a
number of photos, postcards, and letters,
placing them in the trash and/or a box to be
incinerated in the Cary basement. She may
also have left behind a small bundle of
clothes.

Approximately 10:00am - 10:30am: Hazel Drew
departed the Cary residence at Whitman
Court. She then walked to the Harrison residence to see her aunt Minnie Taylor.
According to Minnie, Hazel stated she was
planning to go to Watervliet to meet
friends. Minnie Taylor saw Hazel Drew board
the Pawling Avenue trolley carrying her
dress suitcase, a handbag, and wearing her
nose glasses.

**Undetermined time, approximately
11:00am:** Lawrence Egan and Anna O'Donnell,
working at the W.E. Kerin and Company
grocery store on Congress Street observed
Hazel Drew. Egan stated she was walking west
on Congress Street. Both witnesses confirmed
that Hazel did not have her suitcase at this
time. Kerin's grocery store was located at
106 Congress Street (approximately where the
Vicina Flats are located today.) Walking
westward, Hazel was likely headed directly
for the Union Station, where witnesses later
saw her.

Approximately 11:20am — 11:30am: Witnesses
saw Hazel Drew at Union Station. These
witnesses included Henrietta Robertson,
Lillian Robertson, and Mary Robinson (of
Bedford Street). It is unconfirmed if these

women were at the station as a group. Mary
Robinson stated that she met Hazel at Union
Station and that Hazel said she was taking a
"little trip down the river." Mrs. Henrietta Robertson said she met Hazel at the
station as well, and that she was going
"down the river." Investigators interpreted
this to mean Hazel was planning to go to New
York City. Hazel was seen going to the
ticket window after a train was called.
Witnesses saw Hazel without her suitcase and
carrying a pair of black gloves walking
toward the train platform. Another unnamed
witness may have seen Hazel at this time,
though this unnamed witness was likely
Lillian Robertson whose testimony was deemed
"unimportant" at the inquest.

11:30am: The local train to Albany from Troy
departed Troy, which Hazel may have taken.

12:30pm: The local train to Troy from Albany
departed Albany, which Hazel may have taken.

1:00pm: The Albany to Troy local train
arrived at Troy Union Station.

1:15pm: A girl matching Hazel Drew's
description arrived at the Westcott Express
Company at Troy Union Station and placed an
order to have a trunk collected from the
Cary residence and delivered to the John
Drew residence, Hazel's parents, at 400
Fourth Street in Troy.

2:00pm: Jeanette Marcellus testified that
she saw Hazel Drew at the Troy Union Station

and then spoke to her again shortly after in
the ladies' room at the station.

Troy Record, **Morning and Evening Edition:** An
advertisement ran in the morning and evening
edition of the *Record* stating the following:
"WANTED — Girl for general housework to go
to Sand Lake for summer; references
required. Box 21, Record." Unlike most
other wanted ads that ran that week, this ad
ran for only one day. Investigators theorized this ad may have summoned Hazel to
Sand Lake as she needed new employment
following her departure from the Carys.
Though police investigated, they never
revealed who had run the ad and commissioned
"Box 21" to receive the responses at the
Troy Record.

Evening, approximately 5:00pm: George
Peterson of the Westcott Express Company,
collected Hazel Drew's trunk from the Cary
residence at Whitman Court and delivered it
promptly thereafter to the home of Hazel's
parents at 400 Fourth Street in Troy.
Hazel's mother paid the charges for the
delivery.

Evening, undetermined: A woman with natural
blond hair calling herself "Miss Drew" hired
a stateroom on the steamer *Saratoga*. The
Saratoga traveled overnight from Albany to
New York City. Investigators later performed
a search for women with the Drew surname in
the area who could have made this trip, but
none other than Hazel was ever identified.

July 7, 1908

Early morning, undetermined: If Hazel Drew
traveled to New York City via the steamer
Saratoga, she would have needed to quickly
travel to Grand Central Station and take a
morning train back to Troy to arrive by mid-
morning, as witnesses attested to seeing her.

**Undetermined, possibly between 11:00am and
noon:** Thomas Carey, grocery clerk at W.E.
Kerin and Company grocery store on Congress
Street, stated he saw Hazel Drew on Congress
Street walking toward 5th Avenue. She was
walking on the south side of the street.
Carey stated that he believed she was
carrying a dress suitcase.

1:00pm — 2:00pm: Anna LaBelle witnessed
Hazel Drew in the waiting room of the Troy
Union Station and greeted her with "Hello,
Hazel." Hazel went to the ladies' room and
adjusted her hat in the looking glass.
According to LaBelle she did not have a
suitcase with her at this time.

1:49pm: Adelbert Atwood checked Hazel Drew's
suitcase at the Troy Union Station,
according to station records. This implies
that Anna LaBelle may have encountered Hazel
after her case was checked, as she did not
have it when meeting LaBelle.

After 1:49pm: Hazel Drew likely began her
journey to Averill Park. This would have
required taking a trolley connecting to the

Albia Station, located in the vicinity of
the Terminal Tavern.

**Undetermined, possibly early after-
noon:** Hazel Drew ate her last meal, as
confirmed by her autopsy.

Approximately 3:00-3:30pm: Peter Cipperly
claimed to witness Hazel Drew on the Albia
trolley headed in the direction of Averill
Park in the company of a young man. Cipperly
stated that the woman had blond hair in a
pompadour style. Her hat was off. Cipperly
stated he was certain of the event, as he
kept a diary. However, investigators never
confirmed if Cipperly had witnessed Hazel or
another woman.

Afternoon, undetermined: Dr. Elias B. Boyce,
a Sand Lake native and later part of Hazel
Drew's autopsy team, claimed that he
witnessed Hazel in the Sand Lake area in the
afternoon in the company of a man with a
prominent nose and "receding forehead." As
with the Cipperly testimony, it was never
confirmed if this was Hazel or someone else.

Undetermined: Frank Smith, a 17-year-old
local farmhand who other locals considered
to be a "half-wit" traveled to Taborton to
the farm of a man named Brown regarding
employment. The residence of a "C. Brown" is
listed on contemporary maps, past the
village of Taborton.

No later than 6:15pm: Hazel Drew arrived at
the Averill Park Station on Orient Avenue

and began walking toward the village of
Taborton.

Approximately 6:50-7:10pm: Henry and Charlotte Rollman were traveling down Taborton
Road in the direction of Sliters Corners
when they encountered a girl they believed
to be Hazel Drew walking up the road in the
direction of Taborton. The Rollmans resided
at Bear's Head Mountain, a site to the south
of Crape's Hotel, today located just off NY
Highway 43. The Rollmans stated they met a
girl along the road, above Crape's Hotel (in
the direction of Taborton) and one quarter
mile from where Frank Smith and Rudolph
Gundrum would shortly see Hazel Drew. The
Rollmans claimed the girl was well dressed,
with Mrs. Rollman noting she was impressed
by the girl's hat, as she would like to have
one like it. They also claimed she was
picking and eating raspberries. However, the
doctors found no berries in Hazel's stomach
during her autopsy, so that aspect of the
testimony is suspect.

7:00pm — 7:20pm: Frank Smith departed the
Brown farm. Smith hopped a ride on the wagon
of Rudolph Gundrum, a 35-year-old charcoal
burner, who was driving toward Sliters
Corners. Smith apparently rode in the back
of the wagon. At a spot past Teal's Pond
heading in the direction of Sliters Corners
called "The Hollow," the duo encountered
Hazel Drew. Frank Smith knew Hazel Drew and
later claimed to have said "hello" to her.
Smith and Gundrum were the last people to
see Hazel Drew alive, other than her killer.

From the Hollow, Hazel could have turned north at Taylor's Turn toward her Uncle William Taylor's farm, or south toward Teal's Pond. Either choice would have taken her immediately out of sight of the other witnesses traveling the road that night.

After 7:20pm: Frank Smith and Rudolph Gundrum continued their journey into Averill Park. The duo went to an undetermined saloon, where each had a glass of beer. There is confusion in the contemporaneous press regarding where the duo had their beer. Some sources state it was Harris' Saloon, others Crape's Hotel, though Harris' Saloon seems more likely. Chris Crape stated that Frank Smith arrived at Crape's Hotel around 8:00pm, though this seems unlikely as Smith was witnessed at 9:00pm at the Averill Park train station. Smith eventually finished out the night at Crape's Hotel.

7:15pm — 7:25pm: Hazel Drew was no longer on Taborton Road.

Approximately 7:15pm — 7:25pm: William and Elizabeth Hoffay, who lived three miles beyond Taborton, traveled up the Taborton Road, coming from the direction of Sliters Corners. They encountered Henry and Charlotte Rollman "just beyond Crape's Hotel." At first the Rollmans did not recognize the Hoffays as they were driving a colt rather than the black horse they normally drove. At a further distance in the direction of Taborton, the Hoffays encountered Frank Smith and Rudolph Gundrum at the site of two

chestnut trees. One of these trees appears
to still be standing and is at a spot a
little less than halfway between the Hollow
where Hazel Drew was last seen by Smith and
Gundrum, and Crape's Hotel. Therefore, by
the time the Hoffays encountered Smith and
Gundrum and the Rollmans the latter had
already witnessed Hazel Drew on the road.
The Hoffays did not see Hazel during their
journey to Taborton. However, they claimed
to have seen a runabout carriage parked at
Teal's Pond, which had to pull off the road
for them to pass. According to the Hoffays,
one man was allegedly in the runabout, while
another man was by the pond pulling back the
bushes. While Smith, Gundrum, and the Rollmans confirmed seeing the Hoffays on
Taborton Road that night, no other witnesses
saw the runabout or the two men.

Approximately 7:25pm - 7:30pm: Julia and
Henry Rymiller passed Teal's Pond, traveling
in the direction of Taborton, ahead of Mrs.
Marie Yeabauer also traveling in the same
direction. They claimed to have encountered
Frank Smith and Rudolph Gundrum, heading in
the opposite direction. The *Troy Northern
Budget* stated that they witnessed a girl on
Taborton Road, however other sources stated
that they did not see her. Nor did they see
a wagon at Teal's Pond, as claimed by
William and Elizabeth Hoffay.

7:30pm: Mrs. Marie Yeabauer passed Teal's
Pond traveling toward Taborton, coming from
the direction of Sliters Corners. Mrs.
Yeabauer saw Henry and Charlotte Rollman and

Frank Smith and Rudolph Gundrum by this
time. She did not see Hazel Drew or a
runabout with the two men near Teal's Pond,
as claimed by William and Elizabeth Hoffay,
though based on timing she would have had to
have seen the runabout if it were present
that night.

Approximately 7:36pm: Sunset. New York did
not adopt Daylight Savings Time until 1918.
As such, the sun would have set around
7:36pm local time on July 7th, 1908. Hazel
Drew clearly planned to reach her destination by sunset. Additionally, the moon phase
was a waxing gibbous that night, so some
light would have been cast after moonrise.
Nevertheless, by the time Hazel reached
Teal's Pond, it was dark out.

Approximately 8:10pm: Frank Richmond and his
wife Frederika, along with Frank's brother
Harry, departed the William Taylor farm on
foot for the train station in Averill Park
to see Harry off. They did not witness Hazel
Drew on Taborton Road. They also testified
that she did not come to the Taylor farm
while they were at home.

Approximately 9:00pm: Frank Richmond encountered Frank Smith at the Averill Park
Station. Smith asked Richmond if Hazel Drew
was staying at the Taylor farm and Richmond
informed him that she was not. Harry Richmond, Frank's brother, departed on the
9:00pm train. Following the encounter with
Smith, the Richmonds began walking back to
the Taylor farm. William Taylor testified

that he spent the evening at his farm sitting in a rocking chair and smoking, going to bed around 9:00pm. He stated he did not see Hazel Drew or the Richmonds.

Approximately 10:00pm: The Richmonds arrived at the Taylor farm. They did not encounter Hazel Drew on the road nor was she at the farm. Furthermore, the Richmonds testified they did not see William Taylor until the next morning. Frank Richmond told the local press they encountered a small group of charcoal burners on the road, but that he did not believe they were connected to the murder.

10:15pm: By this time Frank Smith was definitively present at Crape's Hotel where he drank whisky and beer. Smith became friendly with two campers from New York City who were also at the hotel that evening. Smith accepted a wager that he could run to the post office in Averill Park and return within fifteen minutes. He agreed to purchase two postcards to prove his success. Other sources reported that Smith intended to make his run to Dr. Wright's Pharmacy. Either way, when Smith arrived, he found his destination closed and returned to Crape's Hotel without the postcards. He arrived one minute late, losing the bet, which would have placed him back at Crape's Hotel at approximately 10:31pm. Smith spent the rest of his evening at Crape's, including spending time running around a tree to win other wagers, to the amusement of the campers.

Between 11:00pm and Midnight: Frank Smith
departed Crape's Hotel for home. Various
newspapers reported that Frank Smith
departed for home at 11:00pm, while Chris
Crape stated he left the hotel at 11:45. The
later time seems more likely, as Smith spent
some time engaged in wagering and other
antics. Smith was staying with farmer Philip
Brown and family, who did not hear Smith
come home.

Midnight: Mrs. Nennstiel, wife of farmer
William Nennstiel living on Taborton Road
about an eighth of a mile from Teal's Pond,
heard an automobile pass her house, only to
return some time later headed in the direction of the Glass Lake road.

Overnight: Gilbert Miller, camping near
Teal's Pond, heard no sounds coming from the
pond that night. Additionally, Conrad Teal
stated he heard no sounds coming from the
pond.

July 8, 1908

Morning: Frank Smith reported to his mother
that he saw Hazel Drew on Taborton Road.
Frank Smith went to William Taylor's farm
looking for Hazel and was told she was not
there. Smith also called at the farm of
Michael and Libbie Sowalskie, where Hazel's
younger brother Willie Drew was staying, to
see if Hazel was there. She was not. Tom
Sowalskie, the son of Michael and Libbie,
was a giant of a man who was known to be

cruel to farm animals. Smith would later
tell authorities that he was looking for
Hazel Drew as he hoped to "call" on her.
Frank Richmond told William Taylor that he
had heard that Hazel Drew was spotted on
Taborton Road the previous night, but Taylor
seemed unconcerned.

Undetermined time: Minnie Taylor visited the
Drew family home in Troy and asked Hazel's
mother if Hazel was there. She was not.
Minnie then informed Hazel' mother that she
feared Hazel had lost her job.

July 10, 1908

Undetermined time: Lawrence Gruber returned
to his camp at Teal's Pond.

Afternoon: Gilbert Miller saw Hazel Drew's
body floating in Teal's Pond but did not
recognize it as such, believing it to be a
pile of rags.

July 11, 1908

Approximately 9:30am: Lawrence Gruber and
George White witnessed Hazel Drew's body in
Teal's Pond and notified Gilbert Miller. The
body was found floating face down in the
water. Gilbert Miller somehow secured
Hazel's body in the pond before leaving to
contact the coroner in Poestenkill, Morris
H. Strope. Miller telephoned Strope, likely
from the phone at Crape's Hotel.

Approximately 2:30pm: Hazel Drew's body was

removed from the pond by several men,
including Frank Smith, who had arrived at
the pond, and possibly including Gilbert
Miller and Lawrence Gruber. At some point
Miller discovered Hazel Drew's hat and
picked it up. At that time the identity of
the body was unknown. If Frank Smith
suspected it was Hazel, he said nothing.

Dr. Elias B. Boyce, a Sand Lake native, was
the first official on the scene. Before her
body was removed to the undertaker, Dr.
Boyce cut a corset string loose from her
neck. The tightness of the string convinced
him, later on, that she may have been
strangled.

Late afternoon into evening: Coroner Strope
arrived on the scene, possibly traveling in
the same automobile with District Attorney
Jarvis P. O'Brien, Dr. Harry O. Fairweather,
and Detective Duncan Kaye. Strope ordered
the body removed to the Larkin Brother's
Funeral Home in Averill Park, where the
autopsy was performed that night by Boyce,
Fairweather, and Dr. Elmer E. Reichard,
another Sand Lake physician. Detective Kaye
also examined the body. The doctors determined that no water was found in the lungs,
thus Hazel did not drown, and that the cause
of death was from a blow to the head.

Evening: William Taylor went to Crape's
Hotel for a shave. At the hotel Frank
Smith's father told William Taylor that a
body had been found in Teal's Pond, but
Taylor was uninterested.

July 12, 1908

Undetermined time (possibly very late in the day on July 11): John Drew, Hazel Drew's father, read about the discovery of the body in Teal's Pond in the newspapers and went to Larkin Brother's Funeral Home to view the body. He identified the body as Hazel's from the gold filling in her front teeth. It is not known why he suspected the body might be his daughter, though Hazel had clearly gone missing.

Undetermined time: Frank Smith met William Taylor in Averill Park and told Taylor he thought the body in the pond was Hazel Drew. Once again, William Taylor was uninterested. John Drew and one of Hazel's sisters went to the District Attorney's office to view the effects taken from the body and were able to confirm Hazel's identity based on her hatpin and brooch. The pin was a gift from her former employer, Mrs. Tupper. Mrs. Schumacher, Hazel's tailor, and Eva Drew, Hazel's sister-in-law, also viewed the articles removed from the body and were able to identify her by her clothing. Mrs. Schumacher recognized the shirtwaist taken from the body as the one she had stayed up making on the evening of July 3rd. Eva Drew stated she had a skirt made from the same fabric as the one Hazel was wearing.

July 13, 1908

Undetermined time: Detective Duncan Kaye gained access to Hazel Drew's trunk at her

parents' house, discovering her collection
of letters and postcards. Detective Kaye and
Detective William P. Powers, Rennsellaer
County detective, interviewed Mrs. Thomas
Moran at 1019 25th Street, Watervliet and Mrs.
John Rowe at 655 5th Street, Watervliet. These
were allegedly the friends Hazel planned to
visit after departing the Cary residence, as
related by Minnie Taylor. However, neither
had seen Hazel in a month. Mina Jones wrote
to the *Troy Record* requesting copies of
newspapers related to the death of Hazel
Drew.

Mid July 1908

Minnie Taylor wrote to Mina Jones asking her
to destroy all correspondence related to
Hazel Drew.

July 14, 1908

Morning: The Drew family ordered a plot at
the Mount Ida Cemetery in Troy for Hazel
Drew's interment. However, at the last
minute and without explanation, they changed
the location of her burial to the Brookside
Cemetery near Barberville Falls in
Poestenkill, close to where Hazel was born.
A service was held at Larkin Brother's
Funeral Home, presided over by the Reverend
George P. Perry, minister at the First
Baptist Church in Averill Park. This funeral
was attended by Hazel's family, including
William Taylor, and about eight to ten other
mourners. However, Taylor did not attend the
graveside services at the cemetery. He would

later state that he was confused by the
change of venue for the burial. The graveside service was officiated by JHE Rickard
of the Third Street Methodist Church
(Hazel's beloved church). There is confusion
in the press about the funeral services due
to the last-minute change of venue.

Undetermined time: The authorities drained
Teal's Pond in search of clues. Carrie
Weaver's postcard addressed to Hazel Drew
from Carrie's vacation spot in New Carlisle,
Ohio was received at Professor Cary's resi-
dence. The Carys forwarded the card to
Hazel's parents' residence. The *Evening
World* published the "C.E.S." letter.

July 15, 1908

Undetermined time: The newspaper reporters
pressured District Attorney O'Brien to
examine Hazel Drew's clothing. O'Brien and
Detective Duncan Kaye found a nickel in the
tip of Hazel's glove. The County Board of
Supervisors offered a $1000 reward for
information related to Hazel Drew's death.
The reward was heavily publicized in the
following and subsequent days' papers.
The draining of Teal's Pond resulted in no
clues. A handkerchief with the letter "P" on
it was found near the pond but was not
considered to be a clue.

4:00pm: Detective Kaye found Hazel's suitcase at Union Station with the assistance of
Adelbert Atwood who originally checked
the bag.

July 16, 1908

Undetermined time: Carrie Weaver's postcard, forwarded by the Carys, was received at Hazel Drew's parents' house. Mina Jones' letter requesting information related to the death of Hazel Drew was received by the *Troy Record* and immediately published in the paper, making Ms. Jones a subject of interest in the case. The Rensselaer County Sheriff posted notices of the reward on Taborton Road and around Averill Park. Harry Richmond, Frank Richmond's brother, confirmed the facts of Frank's story related to what they witnessed on the night of Hazel Drew's death. Hazel Drew's connection to Edward Lavoie was revealed in the press. Lavoie's sister informed authorities that Hazel feared "a mysterious person." Mina Jones wrote to Minnie Taylor, revealing that Hazel Drew had visited a fortune teller, who told her that she would die that year (1908). John Drew asserted in the press that the handbag found in Hazel's things was not the one she had on her last day. Drew claimed to have seen Hazel on July 4th but was possibly confused about the bag. Minnie Taylor and Julia Drew were also surprised Hazel only had one bag. Carrie Weaver later confirmed that Hazel had lost her second bag while on the girls' recent trip to New York City. The press reported that Minnie Taylor claimed that a second shirtwaist owned by Hazel was missing from Hazel's possessions.

July 17, 1908

Undetermined time: Five anonymous letters were received by District Attorney O'Brien related to the death of Hazel Drew. O'Brien would later reveal these were merely suppositional theories and tales of psychical dreams with no bearing on the case. An anonymous source "working the case" reported to the press that Hazel Drew was despondent and committed suicide. This was never confirmed nor was the source revealed. Another anonymous source (possibly the same as the one above) reported to the press that Hazel was expecting a male friend from New York City. This source may have been William Clemens as it comports with the theories he was advancing and would eventually publish. The Boston chief of police stated publicly that the Boston Police Department was not involved in the Hazel Drew investigation. Boston was a city Hazel had recently visited with Mina Jones. Edward Lavoie, a reference to whom was found in Hazel Drew's things, was notified of Hazel Drew's murder, and reported that their "affair was not serious." Harry Richmond confirmed to authorities that his brother, Frank Richmond, was told by Frank Smith that he had met Hazel Drew on the Taborton Road. Detective Duncan Kaye found Hazel Drew's missing shirtwaist in Hazel's trunk, and he reported that Minnie Taylor was mistaken about it being in Hazel's suitcase. Mina Jones reported publicly that a dentist had asked Hazel Drew to marry her. Mrs. Cary, Hazel Drew's former employer, reported that Hazel had made four trips to Boston, Providence, and New York City while in their employment. Mrs. Cary

also reported that she believed that Hazel
Drew had spent the Independence Day Weekend
in Lake George, but that she believed that
Hazel did not mean any deception in changing
her plans. Mrs. Green, wife of Professor
Arthur Green and Carrie Weaver's employer,
also reported that she believed that Hazel
Drew had gone to Lake George during the
Independence Day weekend.

Afternoon: Authorities asked Mrs. Schumacher, Hazel Drew's tailor, to visit
Hazel's parents' house to determine if any
of her clothes were missing. No follow-up
report was made.

July 18, 1908

Undetermined time: Frank Richmond claimed
publicly that Taborton Road was the most
dangerous road in the county. However, Frank
Smith stated that he believed William Taylor
had told Richmond to say that. Peter
Cipperly of Snyder's Lake came to the
District Attorney's Office to report he had
seen Hazel Drew in the company of a man on
the Albia Car headed to Averill Park around
3:00pm or 3:30pm on the day Hazel died. Mina
Jones reported publicly in a note that Hazel
Drew had a proposal for marriage but could
not remember the man's name. Mrs. Drew,
Hazel's mother, reported that Hazel Drew had
a proposal from a man named Wolf who was
studying to be a lawyer, but that Hazel had
rejected his proposal. It is possible that
the proposal mentioned by Mina Jones and
Hazel's mother were one and the same.

District Attorney O'Brien stated publicly
that he knew who the killer was — an anonymous man from Schenectady with whom Hazel
planned to elope. However, nothing further
ever came of this statement.

July 19, 1908

Undetermined time: Mina Jones stated
publicly that a man working in a dentist
office had proposed to Hazel Drew and that
Hazel Drew could get married any time she
wanted. Mina Jones further stated that Hazel
had been accosted by an Armenian or an
Italian at some point in the past, but that
Hazel had fought him off.

July 20, 1908

Undetermined time: For the first time,
William and Elizabeth Hoffay publicly told
their story of seeing a runabout which
contained two men at Teal's Pond the night
of Hazel Drew's murder. The story was
greeted with some skepticism as it had not
been mentioned earlier and came after the
offering of a reward and the posting of
flyers detailing the reward in their neighborhood. A "club" was found at Teal's Pond
which was widely reported as the murder
weapon. However, others stated that this
club was merely a tree limb. An anonymous
report entered the press that Hazel Drew had
gone to Lake George and New York City,
before her death to meet a young New Yorker
on the mail train. Nothing further came of
this report. The press publicized the post-

cards received from Hazel Drew by William
Hogardt. It was further confirmed that the
"Gordon" mentioned in Hazel's missives was
Gordon Hull. P.J. Shea, a local Troy businessman, offered an additional $500 reward
in silver dollar for evidence related to the
murder of Hazel Drew. The doctors who autop-
sied Hazel Drew revealed publicly that a
contusion caused a blood clot on her brain
that led to Hazel's death. They reiterated
publicly that no water was found in her
lungs confirming she did not drown. Large
crowds of curiosity seekers visited and
explored Teal's Pond and the surrounding
area as the story became more famous. In a
story attributed to William Clemens, police
were allegedly searching for a charcoal
burner overheard to say, "it had to be
done." Minnie Taylor stated publicly that
Hazel Drew had been considering a visit to a
young woman's Christian camp at Altamont,
New York, but police confirmed that Hazel
made no effort to do so. Torn up letters and
postcards were found prepared for incinera-
tion at Professor Cary's house that belonged
to Hazel Drew. William Clemens claimed he
found these items along with a parcel of
Hazel's clothing in the Carys' home.
However, there is no evidence the clothing
was actually present and it appears the
police investigators discovered the letters.

July 21, 1908

Undetermined time: John E. Magner, a Pullman
conductor implicated as a suspect, claimed
publicly that he did not know Hazel Drew.

District Attorney O'Brien confirmed that
Magner — the "railroad man" — had been eliminated as a suspect in the case. Minnie
Taylor stated publicly, however, that Hazel
Drew had met a conductor once and that he
was unable to show her around New York City
due to work commitments. Joseph Drew, Hazel
Drew's brother, stated that Hazel Drew went
driving with a young man the day she was
killed. Nothing further came of this statement, which was never repeated in the press
or at the inquest. Press reported that the
men in the runabout claimed to have been
seen by Mr. and Mrs. Hoffay at Teal's Pond
the night Hazel Drew was killed may have
been fishing for baitfish. Mrs. Julia Drew,
Hazel Drews' mother, stated publicly that
she had engaged a mystic to help solve the
murder, who planned to invoke the spirits
that night.

July 22, 1908

Undetermined time: Dr. Harry O. Fairweather
stated publicly that Hazel Drew's body
showed no signs of abortion or pregnancy.
The press reported that gold bracelets
allegedly missing from Hazel Drew's possessions had been accounted for. One was in
Hazel Drew's trunk and the other was in the
possession of Minnie Taylor. Mr. Hoffay
stated publicly that he had seen William
Taylor in February at Blake's Hotel asking
for a shave and then later in Averill Park
in the company of a light complected, dark-
eyed youngish woman. This could not have
been Hazel Drew as she had blue eyes. James

Able of the livery stable at Averill Park
publicly stated that he had conducted Hazel
Drew to her uncle William Taylor's farm in
April 1908. William Taylor stated that he
had not seen Hazel since February. It would
later turn out that the person witnessed by
Able was likely Stella Karner, who had a
passing resemblance to Hazel Drew, who
visited the Taylor farm with her sister
Kate. The police investigators stated
publicly they were searching for Frank
Jones, husband of Mina Jones, in connection
with the case.

Pullman conductor Magner publicly revealed
that he knew a girl in Troy, but that it was
not Hazel Drew. It was revealed publicly
that Minnie Taylor had asked Mina Jones to
destroy her letters related to Hazel Drew.
Mina stated that she kept three letters and
six postcards, while other mementos were
destroyed during her move to Waterville,
Maine. William Clemens published his infamous story outlining his theory of Hazel
Drew's murder, which paints her as a lasciv-
ious woman leading a double life killed by a
lover. The story appeared in the *Thrice-a-
Week World* and included the letter allegedly
found in Hazel's things from "Harry,"
"Knight of the Napp Kin." Following the
publication of this story it became evident
that Clemens was the person involved in
sensationalizing the case pushing the theory
Hazel was killed by a man or men from New
York City and that she was leading a
dangerous double life.

July 23, 1908

Undetermined time: James Able and A.C. Hogeboom alleged that Hazel Drew and a female friend visited William Taylor after she was supposedly last there in February 1908. As mentioned above these women would turn out to be the Karner sisters. Miss Anna V. LaBelle revealed that she was the friend of Pullman conductor Magner who had been witnessed in his company and that she had given Hazel Drew his address in New York City, with a statement that she told Hazel she should drop in and surprise him. The doctors who performed Hazel Drew's autopsy publicly admitted that Hazel may have died by falling backwards and striking her head.

July 24, 1908

Undermined time: F.W. Schlaffin, a packer from Albany, was revealed publicly to be the subject of a photo found in Hazel Drew's trunk. He stated he had not seen Hazel in a very long time. District Attorney O'Brien dismissed the Hoffay's sighting of the runabout seen at Teal's Pond on the night of Hazel's murder as a serious clue. The investigators began to scrutinize Henry Kramrath and his brother and their camp at Alps, New York, about rumors that were filtering into the press. The two brothers were wealthy businessmen from Albany. Witnesses claimed that wild sex parties were held at the camp and often girls could be heard screaming there.

July 25, 1908

Morning: Samuel LeRoy and his wife were interviewed by District Attorney O'Brien as a result of letters found in Hazel Drew's trunk. O'Brien was searching for a waiter who had worked at Averill Park, a job LeRoy had formerly held. However, he had an iron-clad alibi for the time of Hazel's death.

Undetermined time: Arthur M. Johns, of Burlington, Vermont, stated publicly that a man named Abrams of New York City had killed Hazel Drew. Johns attempted to claim the reward. He was ruled as "probably demented" and dismissed from the investigation. Johns would later have a mental breakdown.

July 27, 1908

Undetermined time: Samuel LeRoy filed suit against the *New York World* newspaper for libel related to their naming him as Hazel Drew's killer. The New York City Chief of Police requested a photo of Hazel Drew from the Troy Chief of Police.

1:00pm: Hazel Drew's inquest began at Warger's Hotel in Averill Park.

July 29, 1908

Undetermined time: Hazel Drew's mother Julia Drew claimed that a prominent man of Troy might have been hypnotized, kidnapped, and murdered Hazel. County detective William P. Powers and Troy City detective Louis Unser

were searching together for clues in the
Taborton Mountains. While District Attorney
O'Brien claimed to have two witnesses who
would state that Hazel Drew was headed in
the direction of Bear's Head Road, nothing
further came of this statement. In addition,
O'Brien stated he was looking into Tom
Sowalskie, who had become known in the press
for his violent temper. Sowalskie never
developed as a suspect.

July 30, 1908

Morning and through the afternoon: Hazel
Drew's inquest was reconvened in the Grand
Jury Room of the Troy Courthouse. Among the
testimony, reporters Louis H. Howe and John
Kelly stated that they found Hazel Drew's
glasses at the base of a stone about two
feet from where her hat and gloves had been
found. Henry Kramrath appeared at the
inquest with an attorney and successfully
repudiated the accusations against him
regarding his camp at Alps. Carrie Weaver
failed to appear as a witness at the inquest
due to her traveling back from Ohio and the
coroner did not keep the proceedings open to
allow her to testify.

July 31, 1908

Coroner Morris H. Strope handed down his
verdict, finding that Hazel Drew was killed
by a blow to the head, but named no
suspects. Following the verdict there were
no additional developments in the case.

Never Answered Questions
Chapter 18

I dreamed about Hazel Drew again, while staying in a cheap one room apartment in downtown Troy and I couldn't figure out how to turn the heat off, so I threw open all the windows to keep from burning up. Hazel visited me, climbing in through the window. She took me for a walk. Her antique Upstate accent was so thick I could barely understand her. She seemed to be, I don't know, checking up on the progress of her case. She walked me to the door of a restaurant and I invited her in for breakfast. But she smiled and said she couldn't go in because it didn't exist in her time.

I woke with a start from the dream before the sun. A crow had perched itself on the open window and its fluttering startled me awake. It was a bitter cold New York February, and I didn't even have a coffee pot in my Airbnb, so I got up and got dressed, following without thinking, the same path Hazel and I had just walked in the dream, down to Manory's Restaurant, which bills itself as the oldest restaurant in Troy. I like to think of it as the real Double R Diner from *Twin Peaks*. Unironically, after taking the first sip of brew, I blurted out, "Damn good coffee!" The case was starting to get to me.

While I was sitting, sipping on my coffee and waiting on my sunny side up eggs and toast, I kept mindlessly scrawling the same phrase over and over again in my notebook: "What were you up to, Hazel?"It's become the mantra for this investigation. What were you up to, Hazel? What, exactly?

I believe that I have established a good understanding of the pivotal events of her life leading up to her death and the context in which she was leading her life, but it's all like looking at a puzzle with most of the center pieces still missing. We are forced to try to imagine the full picture from its fringes alone.

Will Clemens wanted all questions answered, just like in a penny detective story. But uncertainty is a part of reality. Sometimes there are a lot of unanswered questions in life, and we are forced to learn to just sit with that uncertainty. Rather than just let it go or, like Clemens, try to fill in the gaps with fictionalization, I want to explore three of the most crucial of these "never answered questions."

1. Did Hazel Drew Go to Lake George or Schenectady During Independence Day Weekend?

We simply do not know. We know that she spent part of Saturday July 4th in Troy, attending the parade and going to the amusement park. We know that her aunt, Minnie Taylor, claimed that the duo visited the home of Mrs. Annie Weinmann for the remainder of the weekend, and presumably this is what Mrs. Weinmann and her household told investigators. However, we also have evidence from Minnie's attempt to get Mina Jones to destroy her correspondence from Hazel, that Minnie was actively working to cover up...*something*. Mrs. Weinmann was a relative. Aunt Minnie was fiercely protective of her family. It seems possible she pressured the Weinmann household to confirm that Hazel had come to her home Saturday evening and for most of the day on Sunday.

Never mind that Mrs. Cary and Mrs. Green both stated they believed Hazel Drew had gone to Lake George. Never mind that Hazel Drew would not have needed an expensive, custom shirtwaist to hang out at an electric plant worker and a stenographer's house in the lower-class part of town. Is all we know for sure is that Hazel and Minnie departed Troy on the afternoon of July 4th and returned to their homes late in the evening on Sunday July 5th.

In 1908, some of the finest hotels and restaurants in the state of New York were located within immediate walking distance of the Schenectady train station. I tried to track down hotel records from 1908 to determine if Hazel (or one of the suspects) had checked in at such a place, but the records are no longer extant. According to reports, the police made a similar effort, to no avail. However, in 1908, a simple alias would have covered the tracks of two people attempting to stay at a hotel under illicit circumstances. Recall that Chester Gillette and Billy Brown checked into hotels under assumed names.

Maybe Hazel bought her fancy clothes for the sole purpose of walking around Lake George with her maiden aunt. Or maybe, at the last minute, there developed an opportunity for a rendezvous with someone who would have been likewise dressed in fancy attire, a wealthy member of the upper crust. Maybe Minnie's story about a last-minute change of plans was true. But Hazel had been planning the trip for over a month. Everything we know about Hazel Drew indicates that she was never put off easily. What would change her plans would be a chance for a nicer weekend—one for which she suddenly needed those new clothes.

Maybe the Schenectady trip was a cover story made up by Minnie Taylor to hide...something. We have established that Minnie was not above lying, in fact it was her routine in this case. Where Hazel Drew really was throughout the Independence Day weekend remains an unanswered question.

2. Where was Hazel Drew the Night of Monday July 6, 1908

Hazel's movements on the night of July 6th are a true curiosity that leave us open to the potential for a lot of fantasizing. Was she holed up in some luxury hotel with her fancy man and soon-to-be killer? That was a prevailing theory in 1908. Or did she spend the night cruising to New York City aboard the steamer *Saratoga*? We know that "Miss Drew" with natural blond hair booked passage on that ship on July 6th. The police tried to run the clue to ground and discovered that no "Miss Drew" other than Hazel was in a position to be cruising that night.

The *Saratoga* was a ship of the Citizens Line, which plied the Hudson River between Troy and New York City. I found an advertisement in the local newspaper of July 9, 1908, which advertised their rates. A one-way ticket was $1.50, and departure was at 7:30pm. A roundtrip was $2.50. When Hazel's body was found, she was literally down to her last nickel, carried in the fingertip of one of her gloves. Had she traveled to New York and returned via a morning train, it certainly would have wiped out any last wages she was paid, or the money borrowed from her mother, leftover from the weekend.

The investigators offered up other theories about where Hazel stayed the night of July 6th. These included an overnight stay in Albany or the little village of Rensselaer. However, Hazel was not seen going to and from these places, beyond her being sited in and around Troy earlier on the day of July 6th. No friends or relations or hotel desk clerks or restaurant staff ever came forward to confirm Hazel's whereabouts on the night of July 6th beyond the crewman who sold a ticket to "Miss Drew" aboard the *Saratoga*.

We do not know, for certain, where Hazel was on the night of July 6th, but it seems likely she was aboard the *Saratoga*. She had told witnesses at Union Station that she was taking "a little trip down the river." This evidence, coupled to the presence of Miss Drew on the *Saratoga* would seem to confirm that she did exactly that.

3. Was the Troy Record WANTED Advertisement of July 6th Connected in Any Way to the Case?

The following advertisement was run in the morning and evening edition of the *Troy Record* on July 6, 1908 and at no other point before or after: "WANTED—Girl for general house-work to go to Sand Lake for summer; references required. Box 21, Record." Investigators theorized this ad may have summoned Hazel to Sand Lake as she needed new employment following her departure from the Carys. Though police investigated, it was never revealed who had run the ad and commissioned "Box 21" to receive the responses at the offices of the Troy Record.

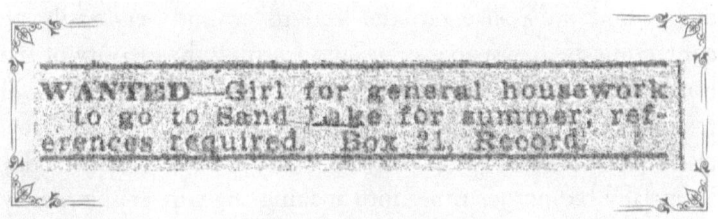

Troy Record, July 6, 1908. Did this advertisement lead Hazel Drew to Teal's Pond?

Prior to the widespread adoption of the telephone, wanted advertisements and "agony" columns in newspapers, which typi-cally ran twice a day, were used for encoded communications.[1] Though telephones had come to Upstate New York by 1908, they were not private. A telephone operator would have likely known which parties were on either end of the call and what the content of the call was, as they were able to listen in quite easily.

Is it possible the ad run in the *Troy Record* was just such an encoded message—a means to summon Hazel Drew to a pre-determined rendezvous point? Had she and another party set up this system of communication well in advance? For those advancing the theory that Hazel was planning an elopement, this seems like the perfect method for triggering the plan.

If Hazel awoke on the morning of July 6th and saw the ad, she would be able to put her plan in motion. Quit her job, clear her possessions from the Cary house, and simply bide her time awaiting the rendezvous at Teal's Pond. She would not have needed money if she were planning to run away, so she could splurge with one last solo trip aboard a steamer. Additionally, if the plan went poorly and her lover did not appear, she needed only walk about a quarter of a mile up the hill to her uncle William Taylor's house for a safe refuge for the night and no doubt a small loan of money to get her home.

This theory fits so well—and it also so fanciful—that it surprises me that Will Clemens did not run with it in the Pulitzer papers.

However, it's every bit as likely the ad was merely a coincidence, and the police ran the lead to ground very easily by contacting the newspaper office and learning the identity of the holder of "Box 21." Barring any further clues, this question will remain forever unanswered. *Something* summoned Hazel Drew to Teal's Pond on the night of July 7, 1908, after she spent a day essentially biding her time until making the trip. If she merely wanted to enjoy the water and the night air, she could have gone on July 6th, after departing the Carys' and spent the night with her uncle and saved her money.

No, whatever brought Hazel Drew to Teal's Pond was meant to take place on July 7th, in the evening, after sunset. Whether Hazel was summoned by a newspaper ad, a telephone conversation, or a prearranged plan, whatever she was planning was meant to play out on July 7th, not July 6th. She had to bide her time for one night before making the trip to Teal's Pond.

What, indeed, was Hazel up to?

[1] Clay, Alice. *The Agony Column of the 'Times.'* London, Chatto and Windus, 1881.

CLOSING THE CIRCLE
CHAPTER 19

I magine that you are sitting in Manory's Restaurant, it's after closing time and we have pulled a few chairs around in a circle and the manager has allowed us to make a final pot of coffee for the evening. I have brought in my "crazy wall" from my study, with pictures, clues, notes, and lines of red thread connecting suspects to one another and to Hazel Drew. Familiar to every mystery aficionado, this is the part of the story where the detective draws all the suspects together to work through each of them, one by one, to try build the case against the killer and, if lucky, force a confession.

Of course, real detective work does not—and has never—worked that way. However, District Attorney Jarvis O'Brien had just such an opportunity at Hazel Drew's official inquest, when the key players were assembled. The Averill Park/Sand Lake/Sliters Corners contingent gathered for a day at Warger's Hotel in Averill Park. The Troy contingent was herded into the Grand Jury Room at the Courthouse, minus one critical witness, Carrier Weaver, who was delayed in her return home from Ohio.

Jarvis O'Brien would have been unfamiliar with the "closed circle" trope in detective fiction; it would not be introduced for another eight years. The trope was invented by the Grand Dame of Murder herself, Agatha Christie, in the novel that birthed her master detective, Hercule Poirot, *The Mysterious Affair at Styles*. Originally Poirot was meant to reveal his killer in a courtroom, at a legal proceeding not unlike the Drew inquest. However, at the urging of her publisher, she moved the action of the reveal to the library at Styles Manor and one of the most successful tools of modern detective fiction was born. O'Brien had that *exact* opportunity. I believe the killer was sitting in the room with him at Hazel's inquest and, unlike Poirot who could methodically tease out the killer's lies and build all the right connections, Mr. O'Brien simply could not. Or did not.

Coroner Morris Strope seems to have had very little role in the inquest, beyond the issuance of his brief ruling, though it was officially Strope's proceeding. It was truly O'Brien's show, and he seems to have lost control of the thing from the beginning. The hearing at Warger's Hotel was an especial circus, with Frank Smith turning up in a starched white shirt and boasting a big cigar, acting like a celebrity boxer, not a suspect in the dock. The anti-Republican press reported gleefully that O'Brien wasn't up to the task. He avoided obvious questions, didn't probe witnesses, and, at the proceedings held int Troy, damn near let Minnie Taylor get off the stand without answering any questions until the members of the press themselves demanded *they* be allowed to grill her. This was a pattern with O'Brien throughout the investigation. Recall the nickel found in Hazel's glove was only revealed after the pressmen demanded her clothing be examined.

The lies and inconsistencies I have pointed out in this book never came up. Despite having mentioned in the press he was close to the killer and even knew the killer, O'Brien never directed the proceedings toward any individual. He never named a suspect and, indeed, at the last minute worked toward a suicide verdict. Early suspects such as Frank Smith and William Taylor were allowed to tell their stories and be dismissed. Much of the testimony was disregarded in the press, literally, as "unimportant."

From the finding of Hazel Drew's body to the handing

down of the coroner's ruling, it had only been *twenty days*. The inquest should have been the start of the investigation into Hazel's murder, not its end. The inquest was convened to find cause of death—to determine how she died. It was clear that officialdom, following that inquest, knew Hazel had been murdered. Yet—POOF—the only legal proceeding ever convened relating to Hazel's death was that inquest. It was the one time in history all the key players were together in a room— that metaphorical library at Style's Manor—in which they could be questioned, cross-examined, and have their stories placed under scrutiny. A fact pattern leading to a killer should have begun to emerge following an analysis of the testimony at that proceeding. We know the New York City police were just getting interested, per the request for a photo of Hazel on July 27th. That would have been on par with Hazel's murder becoming a federal case in terms of investigatory resources in 1908.

But Jarvis O'Brien shut it all down. He stated it would now be time for "private investigators" to pursue leads, hopefully to get paid via the rewards offered. The Troy Chief of Police, who had more-or-less recused himself from the entire investigation, did not pursue the case. Sheriff J. Irving Baucus, whose jurisdiction Hazel's case really belonged to, did not continue the investigation. Beyond posting reward flyers, his primary contribution to the case appears to have been urging O'Brien to figure out a way to mark the thing down as suicide.

Jarvis P. O'Brien did his job, if we define that job as getting Hazel Drew in the ground, papering her murder with a basic legal proceeding, and putting her death in the community's rearview mirror. After July 31 the case went cold—*ice cold*. No more coverage, no more investigation, literally nothing for almost eighty years, as the citizens of Rensselaer County walked and talked and engaged with one another, allowing the whole thing to disappear from memory until the very last witnesses had died.

It cannot be overstated how unusual this is for unsolved crime—especially a crime like Hazel Drew's—so we are forced to believe, in the end, that a part of District Attorney O'Brien's job was to *make* the whole thing go away. O'Brien himself told the press that he had been "forced" to accept that Hazel was murdered by the doctors who performed the autopsy, and that otherwise he was willing to chalk her death up to suicide. As we shall shortly see, he tried to wedge this theory into the inquest as well, even after his investigation. In the same way that Will Clemens was no Sherlock Holmes, O'Brien was no Hercule Poirot—despite having a mustache that would rival that of the Belgian detective. He was what he was—a machine politician beholden to a system of masters greater than himself. That's exactly how he behaved.

As we proceed through this list of suspects, we must keep that in mind. We are not only putting potential murderers under scrutiny, but we are also scrutinizing the investigators. So, I have gathered you here to our metaphorical seats in Troy's oldest restaurant, with cups of damn fine coffee in hand, to reveal a killer. One by one we shall go through the most likely suspects. These are the suspects presented by the contemporary authorities as well as suspects raised by modern investigators. I intend to play fair here—no mysterious third parties will be introduced. I will not scrutinize left field theories or engage in ungrounded speculation. Hazel Drew was killed by a human being who played a very real role in her life. This person gave testimony at her inquest and, if O'Brien's men had wanted to make it so, should have been the subject of serious inquiry.

Pour yourself a cup of coffee and let's get going. It's time to close the circle.

THE SUSPECTS

CHAPTER 20

THE SUICIDE THEORY

This is the theory the official investigators seemed to prefer, from the very start of the case. Throughout the twenty days of the investigation, the suicide theory was never far from the pages of both the local and national press. The papers reported that someone "close to the case" revealed that Hazel Drew was unlucky in love, despondent, and killed herself. The presence of her hat and gloves, neatly placed along the cow trail leading down to Teal's Pond, were supposedly indicators of someone getting themselves organized to take their own life.

Suicides will do exactly this; jumpers, for instance, will often remove their shoes. It is not uncommon to find personal effects such as wallets and the contents of pockets, neatly organized next to a suicide victim. However, the more astute members of the media immediately countered this, by arguing that Hazel's things had been staged to look like suicide.

HAZEL DREW MYSTERY LIKELY TO END WITH VERDICT OF SUICIDE

Expert Introduced at Inquest Does
Not Agree With Doctors Who Per-
formed Autopsy and Coroner
May Accept Theory of Suicide.

*Evening World, July 27, 1908. Until the end, Jarvis P.
O'Brien pushed the theory that Hazel Drew committed
suicide.*

District Attorney Jarvis P. O'Brien seemed almost *desperate* to
chalk Hazel's murder up to suicide. On July 20, 1908, it was
widely reported in the press that O'Brien was willing to accept
the suicide theory had it not been for the verbal report of the
physicians' autopsy of Hazel Drew, which had just been made
public. The key factors in that determination were the fact that
Hazel died from head trauma, not drowning. She had no water
in her lungs.

However, at the very last possible moment, D.A. O'Brien called
another medical man to the stand, whose name was reported in
the press as Dr. C.B. Herrick. This could be none other than Dr.
Clinton Bradford Herrick, a very well-trained surgeon with resi-
dency status at the Troy Hospital. He was a good Irish
Methodist from a prominent Troy family who moved in the
same social circles as O'Brien and all of Hazel's former employers. Herrick's expertise was a "railway surgeon"— he even wrote
an authoritative text on the subject in 1899 and, like O'Brien,
seems to have made his primary income off working for the railroads. In the nineteenth and early twentieth centuries, railway
surgery was a full-blown discipline of medical science, concerned
with everything from treating patients aboard moving trains, to
the medical response to railway accidents. However, one word

never mentioned in his authoritative text on the topic is "suicide."[1]

Dr. Herrick was a trained surgeon and possibly one of the best trauma surgeons in the country at the time he gave his testimony in 1908. However, he was not a general practitioner nor was he a forensic investigator. Outside of his expertise as a trauma surgeon, his opinion that Hazel Drew committed suicide was not that of an expert. Factoring in that he did not examine the body it seems more likely that we should defer to the expertise of the three medical men— all of whom would have had to deal with suicides in their profession— as to her cause of death.

It is tempting to believe that D.A. O'Brien, as a Hail Mary pass to influence the coroner's ruling, called on one of his railroad cronies to offer a dissenting medical opinion. To die by drowning, Hazel merely needed to throw herself into the mighty Hudson River and allow its quick current to drag her under. For Hazel to die by suicide at Teal's Pond she would have had to neatly arrange her hat and gloves, somehow lose her glasses, walk out on the stone dam at the pond in the dark, jump off, hit her head, and die before going into the water. This chain of events is preposterous. In fact, it's so preposterous we must ask ourselves why a professional like Jarvis O'Brien kept trying to argue for a version of this exact narrative.

Hazel Drew did not die by suicide.

THE AUTOMOBILIST

Beyond murder or suicide, the Troy authorities considered and dismissed the idea that Hazel Drew was killed in an accident: she had merely slipped and fallen into Teal's Pond. Due to what we know about the placement of her fallen glasses, it is safe to say even if she did die as the result of a fall, *someone* placed her in Teal's Pond. An early theory that emerged and which was offered by the police was that Hazel Drew was killed by a careless motorist, he tossed her into Teal's Pond and then staged a scene to make it seem like a suicide.

At this point in 1908, automobiles were still rare, though their popularity was growing. Henry Ford would not release his mass market Model T until November of that year and, as a result, cars were still largely a thing owned and operated by the upper crust. Laws were minimal and protections for pedestrians were limited. Accidents—and attempts to cover them up—were very much a phenomenon when Hazel Drew was killed.

Recall that Chris Crape spied an automobile on Taborton Road either the night of Hazel's death or the night before that belonged to Harold D. Neach. Another witness, Mrs. Nennstiel, witnessed a car going to and from the direction of Teal's Pond at about midnight on July 7th.

District Attorney O'Brien, who himself arrived on the scene in a car, had some conflicting things to say about an automobile and Hazel's death. Though investigators reported in the press on July 18th it was possible a motorist had killed Hazel, O'Brien himself stated that he did not believe a car could make it up Taborton Mountain. Yet, O'Brien himself seems to have made the drive, as did Mr. Neach and whomever it was driving around at midnight when Hazel died. It seems likely, once again, that O'Brien was looking to throw the scent off the "great and the good" of Troy —the people who could afford to buy a car in 1908.

I am certain that Hazel's killer arrived and departed in an auto-mobile. In fact, I believe the killer arrived and departed in that very same automobile witnessed by Mrs. Nennstiel. However, Hazel was not killed *by* an automobile, and we know this because of her autopsy. The doctors stated firmly that beyond the contusion on Hazel's head, she had no other wounds or damage to her body. Had she been hit by a car, even if the cause of death was head trauma, damage from the accident would have been present on her body.

Hazel Drew was not killed in an automobile accident.

THE SOLDIER

It was immediately assumed that if Hazel Drew were murdered it was by either a lover or someone whose affections she spurned. Among those potential suspects stands Edward Lavoie, a young man who began his career as a baker but joined the army in 1900. When Hazel Drew's suitcase was discovered by authorities and examined, it contained a personal advertisement from a local paper that stated that Mr. Lavoie was traveling to Chattanooga, Tennessee. The advertisement was dated October 23, 1907. Hazel herself wrote the date October 6, 1907, on the ad and clearly retained it as a keepsake.

Ron Hughes lays out the case against Edward Lavoie in summary: if William Clemens is to be believed and Hazel Drew retreated to her uncle William Taylor's farm to have an abortion after leaving the Tupper residence, the date of October 6, 1907 would have been just about the time Hazel could have become pregnant with Soldier Lavoie's child. Hearing the news, Lavoie became enraged, set up a meeting with Hazel, and killed her.[2] However, this is highly unlikely as Mr. Lavoie was almost certainly not in Troy as he was tied up with his military duties. When his name first appeared in the press, neither Lavoie's uncle nor sister could account for his whereabouts, though it is clear that his family knew Hazel Drew. Lavoie's sister made the statement that Hazel feared a strange man and I believe she may have been the female friend that Hazel was seen with by Mr. Magner when she visited his boarding house in New York City.

Edward Lavoie, according to extant records, joined the army on February 26, 1900, and served for three years in Company H, Seventh Cavalry, spending time in Cuba. He was discharged in 1903. In 1907 Lavoie decided to re-enlist. Though a Watervliet native, at the time he rejoined the service, his address was listed as New York City and he was working as a time clerk.

Therefore, it seems likely that October 6, 1907, was the last time Hazel Drew saw Edward Lavoie. October 6, 1907, was a *Sunday*, so it stands to reason that this encounter may have taken place at church, in keeping with Hazel's tendency to meet men at church or for them to accompany her to services. Perhaps Lavoie made a last visit to see friends and family in Troy before re-enlisting. Lavoie re-enlisted on October 25, 1907, at Fort Slocum in New York City and was mustered into Company L, Twelfth Cavalry. The newspaper advertisement was dated October 23rd, so it

seems likely Mr. Lavoie changed his mind about going to
Tennessee. Prior to 1911, the Twelfth Cavalry was stationed at
posts in Texas, Georgia, and the Philippines. When Lavoie was
discharged from the army on October 10, 1910, that was at Fort
McDowell, California. Fort McDowell was a primary station for
processing Americans sent to and from deployments in the
Pacific. This means that Mr. Lavoie was almost certainly posted
to the Philippines, where Twelfth Cavalry had a major presence.
Lavoie's uncle, Edward Rice, stated that he thought that his
nephew had a posting somewhere "up north," but this isn't
possible – his unit didn't have a presence in the north. Rather it
is most probable that by the time Hazel Drew was killed, Lavoie
was at Fort Oglethorpe, Georgia getting ready for his eventual
overseas deployment. Authorities did eventually track Lavoie
down and they eliminated him as a suspect; his relationship with
Hazel Drew was casual.

Nevertheless, O'Brien's men made every attempt to connect
Lavoie's movements to Hazel's trips to New York and Boston,
without success. At the time of his enlistment, Lavoie was living
at 105 West 52nd Street in New York City, which astute observers
will note is the modern address of the Museum of Modern Art.
It is thus *entirely* possible that Edward Lavoie was a part of Hazel
Drew's NYC friend circle. Even if he had gone off to the army,
she may have known people in town connected to him, such as
his sister.

A relationship between Hazel Drew and Edward Lavoie is only
important if it could lead to her death. It seems clear that Lavoie
was in the service at the time Hazel was killed in July. If he had
leave to visit Troy in July, he came and went utterly unnoticed.
His friends and family didn't see him, nor could they account
for his whereabouts. Nor was such a man seen wandering about
Sand Lake. It is clear that when tracked down by authorities,
Lavoie had an alibi sufficient to clear his name, likely due to his
military service.

The soldier, Edward Lavoie, did not kill Hazel Drew.

THE CONDUCTOR

This case is a Tale of Two Conductors; however we know from his own efforts to clear his name, that one of the two Pullman men, Samuel LeRoy, was not guilty. He was drawn into the case merely because he had once worked as a waiter in Averill Park and was confused with John E. Magner, whose New York boarding house address was found in Hazel Drew's things. Mr. LeRoy is out of the circle, so let's look at Mr. Magner.

Magner clearly knew Miss Anna V. LaBelle, though the nature of their relationship is unclear. I suspect Miss LaBelle was very much a character in line with that of Minnie Taylor. After a job in her youth as a buttonholer in a collar factory, LaBelle spent the rest of her working life at the job she had when she knew Hazel Drew: a saleswoman in a department store.

She never married and she lived in a series of lodging houses at Watervliet, Green Island, and along the Hudson in Troy within easy distance of her employers. She died in 1948 at a ripe old age, having never decided to take on a male partner. It seems likely that whatever game Minnie and Hazel were up to in 1908, Anna LaBelle was playing it similarly with the likes of Mr. Magner, whose New York address she provided to Hazel Drew, and whom Hazel decided to visit, by Magner's admission. Word had likely gotten round that Magner was a soft touch for a pretty girl.

We simply do not know what John Magner and Hazel Drew got up to on her trip to New York City. Though she was there with another girl, Carrie Weaver was adamant that this was not her. This implies Hazel had a connection in New York which was never fully disclosed. Whether Hazel was turned away just as Magner said or whether they had a night out on the town is irrelevant. Though it would be problematic for Magner to lie as the other girl with Hazel, were she to turn up, could undermine his story. So, it seems likely that his primary focus was LaBelle, and he did, in fact, turn Hazel and her counterpart away. This would also explain why Hazel saw no value in keeping Magner's address.

The more lurid press continually hinted that Hazel was planning an elopement to New York City at the time of her death.

Though that seems highly unlikely as she had made no plans to leave the Cary home prior to at least Sunday night, when she returned from her holiday weekend. She had agreed to see Carrier Weaver off to Ohio on Monday morning, a plan which was abandoned with no notice. If Hazel had a lover in NYC, the impromptu trip to that city to track him down on July 6th might make sense.

Let us suppose Hazel Drew took an evening boat to New York City to meet Magner. She would have had to barge into his home at the crack of morning and convince him to come to Troy with her or book a ticket on his train so they could have a conversation. Both Hazel and Magner lived in Troy so the choice of Teal's Pond for this liaison is odd for them (as it would be, frankly, for any of our suspects). However, Hazel may have wanted to meet to sort out their relationship on "home turf" – close to her uncle, but away from prying eyes.

If that man were John Magner, like Hazel, he had to get to Teal's Pond. Hazel was witnessed traveling there. The county authorities checked all the places in the city where a horse and trap could be rented and Magner was never connected to a horse rental. Remember, that in July 1908 Henry Ford had not yet introduced the Model T, so cheap cars were still a few months in the future. Magner was a coachman; he simply could not afford a car. Magner's challenge in killing Hazel Drew—like a lot of our suspects—would be getting to and from Teal's Pond without being seen, in the dead of night, *via public transportation*.

The contemporary investigators found no connection between the between Hazel and John Magner that was noteworthy and Magner himself would have certainly been witnessed traveling to and from Teal's Pond. Magner was LaBelle's friend, not Hazel's. Magner had a sufficient alibi to take the focus off him, while the Pulitzer papers went down the rabbit hole of accusing our other Pullman coachman, Samuel LeRoy, of doing the murder. But neither man had the means and opportunity – even if we could imagine a motive – to kill Hazel Drew at Teal's Pond without leaving a trace.

The Conductor, John Magner, did not kill Hazel Drew.

THE CAMPERS

In a case crippled by distractions, one of the most frustrating, but tantalizingly lurid, was the suspicion cast on a hunting camp near Alps, New York. The camp was owned by two wealthy brothers from Albany, New York, Henry E. and Alexander Kramrath, with Henry being the primary focus of the suspicion. The camp was notorious by the time Hazel was killed, the subject of considerable local gossip. The two men were suspected of running their camp as a brothel. News reports from the time indicate they had paid out hush money to at least one local girl to cover up their illicit activities.

Suspicion was thrown on the Kramraths late in the investigation by Detectives Powers and Unser, who had dedicated their efforts toward chasing down leads local to Taborton Mountain. On July 23, 1908 they took down a report from a local named Minnie Clifford, who lived near the camp, who claimed that on July 6th or 7th she heard a woman's scream emanating from the camp, followed later by the sound of a passing car.

CLEWS LEAD NOWHERE

Inquest Fails to Solve the Hazel Drew Mystery.

RUMORS ABOUT CAMP DENIED

Rich Man of Albany Questioned About Stories of Women's Screams Heard From His Place in Woods—Witnesses Corroborate Him—Night Visit of Auto to Scene of Murder Explained.

She further stated that this was part of a pattern of strange behavior related to the spot. In early May 1908 allegedly two women appeared at the camp with the intention to stay for a while. One of the girls – the younger – was described by Clifford as looking like Hazel Drew. According to Clifford, this girl came to her farm to buy butter and reported that she was staying at the camp with her aunt. This was implied in the press to be Hazel and her Aunt Minnie Taylor. It was further stated by Clifford that this girl appeared again at her farm and begged Mrs. Clifford to take her into town, as she had a Decoration Day trip planned and was also planning to travel to Lake George. Immediately this story raises red flags because it was made relevant to authorities *well after* the various rewards related to Hazel's murder had been offered and posted on signs in the area by the county Sheriff. The story related to Hazel's travels around Decoration Day and her plans to go to Lake George over the Independence Day weekend were in the press, where Clifford could have received the information needed to pad out her story. Obviously, Hazel was not staying at a camp in May 1908 with her aunt as their movements during this time are accounted for. The Cary's gave her leave for the long Decoration Day (Memorial Day) weekend and that was it. Even her late return on Sunday with Carrie Weaver had to be explained to her employers. Yet it is clear the Kramraths were up to *something* at their camp and had created a lot of bad blood in the area.

The camp itself was called Tsatsawassa and was located in Dunham Hollow, not far from the town of Alps. The Cliffords had been caretakers at the camp and clearly weren't fans of the owners. Mabel Brown, proprietor of Brown's Hotel on Glass Lake (haunt of the illustrious Theodore Roosevelt) seemed to confirm the story. She stated that the younger of these women appeared at her hotel asking to use the phone so she could call for a doctor to assist her aunt. When the call was made, Brown recognized the recipient as one of the Kramraths. Supposedly the two women later returned to Brown's Hotel requesting the phone once again, this time so they could call a ride to take them home.

It is certain that Hazel Drew and Minnie Taylor were not the women summering at this camp at Alps. But could Hazel have been there the night she was murdered? Unlikely, simply because of the distance. The distance between Teal's Pond and

Dunham Hollow is between 6-7 miles depending on the path taken. Were Hazel trying to get to the camp, she would not have gone to Teal's Pond, she would have turned south at Sliters Corners and walked past Glass Lake and Brown's hotel. However, we know she was at Teal's Pond by sunset. To get to Alps and the camp, someone would have had to pick Hazel up, take her there, and then, for some reason, kill her at that site and then dump her body back at Teal's Pond. The evidence of Hazel's glasses precludes this, because it seems obvious that she lost those in the fall that killed her.

So why were Henry and Alexander Kramrath placed under suspicion? Obviously, at the outset, Clifford and Brown thought it was "safe" to cast aspersions on the two men, who, to be fair, were not innocents. When District Attorney O'Brien was questioned about the accusations, he told the press flat out that his office didn't tolerate that kind of business "on this side of the river." Keeping in mind that Mame Faye was running the most infamous sex trade in the state a couple of blocks from the D.A.'s office, that statement itself is absurd. O'Brien had made his name as a reformer shuttering a few brothels and the like, but it seems this was to make a safe space for controlled businesses like Mame Faye's, which were sanctioned by the local establishment. Being part of that establishment led to protection. Clifford and Brown were summoned to the inquest to provide testimony related to their experiences. They were among the last to testify, possibly in anticipation of fireworks, of which there were none. Henry Kramrath himself testified last or next to last at the inquest. He, however, did something none of the other witnesses did – he appeared on the stand in the company of a lawyer, John A. Stephens. Rather like Samuel LeRoy, it was not Kramrath's intention to be taken down by gossip and yellow journalism. Attorney Stephens was no small fry in the profession, he was a law partner of David B. Hill, former Governor and Senator from New York and served as Hill's personal attorney. However, Hill—and almost certainly Stephens and Kramrath, were *Democrats*. O'Brien and his cronies were part of the Republican machine—as would have been a hotelier playing

host to President Roosevelt. The Kramraths were on the wrong
side of the river politically as well.

Kramrath appeared on the stand loaded for bear. He and his
lawyer provided meticulous alibis accounting for his movements,
establishing his presence in Albany on the night of July 7th.
While the Kramraths may have been up to no good, it was
immediately clear that they were not involved in the death of
Hazel Drew and that the accusations thrown at them were
unsubstantiated. Hazel and Minnie were not at Alps in May of
1908 and the physical evidence makes it clear that Hazel died at
Teal's Pond. She was not transported there and back.

The Campers, Henry and Alexander Kramrath, did not kill
Hazel Drew.

THE DENTIST

Multiple witnesses asserted that Hazel Drew had an acquaintance in a dentist's office who was romantically interested in her.
The press—and some subsequent researchers—have erroneously
concluded that this person *was* a dentist. This led to a lot of
confusion in 1908, and that confusion persists.

Hazel Drew took her health seriously, including her teeth. She
had dental work done already by the age of 20. Her dentist was
almost certainly Dr. Edward J. Knauff, whose office and residence were at 49 Third Street in Troy. The location of his office
fits Hazel's shopping pattern – the Boston Store and her
optometrist were also nearby. Dr. Knauff confirmed that he had
seen Hazel as a patient.

We know that in the weeks leading up to her death, Hazel
appeared at Knauff's office requesting an evening appointment
and he told her he did not offer them. According to Mrs. Cary,
Hazel asked her if she could visit the dentist in the evening and
Mrs. Cary, finding this irregular, told her no. If Hazel had asked
the dentist for an evening appointment and was told *no* before
asking Mrs. Cary's permission, then then there was no need to
ask for Mrs. Cary's permission. And vice versa—no reason to ask
Dr. Knauff for an evening appointment if her employer would

not allow her to go to one. It seems more likely that Hazel Drew was fishing around for an excuse to be hanging around Dr. Edward Knauff's office after hours. That reason, perhaps, was not Dr. Knuaff, but his son William, a student at Rensselaer Polytechnic Institute only slightly older than Hazel herself.

The contemporary press was quick to propose an affair between Hazel and Dr. Knauff. When Hazel was supposedly seen by witnesses at Kerin's Grocery Store walking up Congress Street, Dr. Knauf, who was present at the time, later claimed it was not her. He also claimed that he saw this woman board the Albia car later in the day on July 6th and that it was not Hazel Drew. Whether or not this was or was not Hazel Drew, Dr. Knauff felt certain that he knew Hazel well enough to recognize her.

Dr. Knauff was asked flat-out if he and Hazel were having an affair. The 49-year-old dentist denied it. So, we must go back to exactly what was said about Hazel Drew and her dentist office lover. The press reported that Mina Jones "said that Hazel often made reference to a friend who worked in a dentist's office in Troy, but never mentioned his name."[3] This man, according to Mina, was "anxious" to marry Hazel.

Hazel had in play three potential suitors – the man who dumped her when she got sick, the future attorney named Wolf (who she seemed not to care for), and this person at the dentist office. We know that one trait of Hazel's potential suitor is that she met him at church. However, Hazel was a devout Methodist and the Knauffs were Episcopalian. Additionally, though William Knauff was a dentist's son and resided in an office alongside his father's practice, he himself did not appear to work there. He was an engineering student at RPI.

Careful investigation leads us to discover that William Knauff never graduated RPI but that he did go on to practice civil engineering as a career. This means it is almost certain that William Knauff was a student of Professor Cary's, Hazel's final employer. This tightens their potential circle even more. He was her dentist's son, and he may have appeared at the Cary home for drinks or a meal, as a student. This gives plenty of opportunity for the two to encounter each other and spark up a relationship.

Or it's entirely possible that if Hazel Drew knew William Knauff prior to her illness it was through *him* that she found employment with Professor Cary. Either way, these three individuals were moving in a very close circle to each other. In a rather curious turn of events, however, this also makes it surprising that Mrs. Cary could not remember Hazel's dentist's name—when that dentist was almost certainly the father of one of Cary's students.

At first it seems easy to dismiss either Knauff as a suspect in the case. While either man might have the motive, the means and opportunity are elusive at first glance. However, due some masterful detective work on the part of Ron Hughes we learn that Knauff had another abode besides the one on Third Street and that it had a stop on the Albia Car—the very car that Hazel was riding to her final destination at Averill Park.[4] The Albia Car had 28 stops between the Albia Station and Averill Park, with Averill Park being number 28. The 10th stop was "Dr. Knauff's" and the 11th was the Five Cent Fair Limit for a ride. Recall that when Hazel's body was examined, she still had a nickel in her glove that would have covered a ride back to "Dr. Knauff's" stop on the Albia line. Ron Hughes supposes that Hazel and William Knauff could have been planning an elopement and that the two rendezvoused at the dentist's country cabin on July 6th, where Hazel spent the night. The following day, a quarrel ensued, and Hazel made her way to Teal's Pond, in the vicinity of her uncle's house, where Knauff the Younger caught up to her and, during a quarrel, killed her and dumped her into the pond. Feeling remorse, he eventually failed out of RPI and moved away to start a new life.

Hughes has presented a good theory and one we need to take seriously, but it has a couple of problems. First it supposes that Dr. Knauff recognized Hazel on the Albia car but suspected his son and gave testimony that the girl he saw was not Hazel. That makes no sense—if Knauff suspected his kin of the murder, he never even had a need to speak up about seeing Hazel in the Albia car. Why draw suspicion in order to dismiss it? Secondly if Hazel Drew were fleeing the Knauff home near

Snyder Lake but did not have the funds to return to Troy, why would she go to Teal's Pond? She could have called a friend or relative in Averill Park to come get her. In addition, her uncle William Taylor literally *lived across the street* from Teal's Pond. Her stroll up Taborton Road was casual, Hazel was not in flight. There was intense interest in Dr. Knauff as a suspect in the press. However, the alibi he was able to provide to the authorities was sufficient for them to not take him—or his family—seriously at the inquest. That does not, however, mean that the Knauffs— especially William—did not know *considerably* more about Hazel Drew and her relationships than was presented at the time. A lot of questions were simply never asked, especially regarding Knauff's relationship with Hazel Drew and her employer. We know Hazel and Minnie were seen riding around with friends in Averill Park, though we don't know who these friends were. The Knauffs? They were in the area.

Of the potential witnesses who went uninvestigated, William Knauff is arguably the most frustrating. Did he know Hazel Drew? Were they lovers? We do not know.

However, the dentist, Dr. Edmund Knauff did not kill Hazel Drew. It is likely his son did not kill her either.

THE CORRESPONDENTS

This is the collection of suspects I care to deal with the least. It seems clear that someone who knew Hazel Drew killed her. The question is, was that "someone" one of the men whose letters were contained in her trunk, or the torn scraps found in the Cary basement? From what little we know about her correspondents they seem to be acquaintances of Hazel's that had fairly innocent relationships with her. Mr. William Hogardt, of Dead- ham, Massachusetts, was Hazel's last man friend to spend a lot of time trying to cultivate a relationship with her, even after Hazel Drew's correspondence with him had trailed off. Her rela- tionships with these letter writers were largely innocent. She met men as any young girl would and took them on innocent dates, notably to church. Of her correspondents, the one she seems to have had the most interest in was the fellow Gordon Hull, for whom Hazel complained she'd lost touch with.

I am also skeptical of the letter writers as suspects because Minnie Taylor made no effort to conceal *their* letters. Presumably she knew Hazel's social circle and the person to who she reached out to ,with a request to destroy letters, was not a *man*, but Mina Jones. Minnie's only worry regarding Hazel's other friends was that they might be drawn into the case unfairly.

Not to spoil another investigator's thesis, we must consider the correspondents as suspects largely because of the work of Ron Hughes, author of *Who Killed Hazel Drew?* Of his suspects, he leans most heavily upon the mysterious letter writer C.E.S., a portion of whose letter was published by Will Clemens in the July 14, 1908 edition of the *Evening World*. I have two leading problems with C.E.S. as a suspect. While Clemens stated Hazel had in possession six letters by this person, none of them were referenced by any reporter *other* than Clemens as a primary source.

Clemens' own contemporaries knew better than to trust his reportage—he'd been caught fabricating things before – so they did not echo his stories. David Bushman and Mark T. Givens, authors of *Murder at Teal's Pond*, dismiss the second Clemens letter, supposedly signed by the Knight of the Napp Kin, published on July 22, 1908, in the *Thrice a Week World* as authentic and I tend to agree. The similarities between it and the C.E.S. letter incline me to dismiss them both.

Hazel's correspondence paints a different picture entirely, not of a girl madly crafting love letters in the vein of Billy Brown, but of a woman pulling away from letter writing. Whereas once she had been in regular correspondence with the lovelorn Hogardt, she cut him off in April 1908. Hazel's arrival at the Cary residence seems to have marked a period of retreat in Hazel's life. She was focusing on travel, spending time with her aunt Minnie, and as reported by many witnesses, doing a lot of reading. There's no place in her schedule, as the C.E.S. letter implies, for a torrid love affair carried in Albany taverns.

The named correspondents did not kill Hazel Drew.

THE STRANGER

Early suspicion in the death of Hazel Drew was that she was killed by a stranger. Lurid reports by Clemens recount the alleged story of a mysterious man presenting himself at Crapes' Hotel for a belt of hard liquor, mumbling something about "it had to be done." Taborton Road had a rough reputation. Charcoal Burners worked the mountain day and night and a crowd of them were witnessed walking into town on the night Hazel was killed.

The theory that Hazel was killed by strangers requires one of three motives: 1) she was killed in a "hit" to silence her, 2) she was killed in a robbery, 3) she was killed and sexually assaulted. Everyone in 1908, right up to the last minute of the inquest, had assumed that Hazel had been bludgeoned over the head with a stick or a rock. It was at the bitter end that the doctors admitted she could have fallen and hit her head, only to be tossed into the pond post-mortem.

As a result, we can dismiss the theory that Hazel was killed by a hitman. An assassin would have used a weapon, not relied on the random possibility of a fall. We can also dismiss the other two motives, robbery and sexual assault. Hazel Drew had little of value to steal – she had one nickel in her glove and the few pieces of jewelry on her body were left alone. Likewise, the doctors who performed her autopsy made it clear that Hazel was not sexually assaulted. She had no other injuries on her body, indicating an attack. This rules out sex crazed charcoal burners or the violent Sowalskie boy, who, as mentioned in our timeline, fell briefly into the frame at the end of the investigation.

A random stranger, though they might have had a means and opportunity to kill Hazel Drew, likely would not have had the motive. A hitman would not have relied on death via a slip and fall. It becomes ever clearer that Hazel's death was not random – but it wasn't premeditated either. It was done by a killer who knew enough to try to make it look like a suicide, but not enough to be successful. Hazel Drew knew her killer and, it is certain, went to Teal's Pond to meet them.

Hazel Drew was not killed by a stranger.

THE RUNABOUT

No murder mystery would be complete without a red herring. William and Elizabeth Hoffay's entry into the story created considerable distraction late in the case, which the press pinned a lot of hope on. On July 15th, the Rensselaer County leadership appropriated a $1000 reward for evidence related to Hazel's murder. The next day the county sheriff posted notices of the reward up and down Taborton Road. A handful of days later, on July 20th the Hoffays came forward with a story regarding the night of Hazel's murder. They, too, claimed to be part of the traffic jam on Taborton Road in the last minutes before sunset on that hot Tuesday night.

The Hoffays lived three miles beyond the village of Taborton and were on the road that night coming from the direction of Sliters Corners. They encountered Henry and Charlotte Rollman "just beyond Crape's Hotel." At first the Rollmans did not recognize them as they were driving a colt rather than the black horse they normally drove. At a further distance in the direction of Taborton, the Hoffays stated that they encountered Frank Smith and Rudolph Gundrum at the site of the two chestnut trees, one of which still exists. This tree stands a little less than halfway between the Hollow where Hazel Drew was last seen by Smith and Gundrum, and Crape's Hotel.

The Hoffays did not see Hazel during their journey to Taborton. However, their presence on the road that night was confirmed by other witnesses. The couple claimed to have seen a runabout carriage parked at Teal's Pond, which had to pull off the road for them to pass. According to their testimony in the press, one man was allegedly in the runabout, while another man was by the pond, pulling back the bushes. A runabout is a very lightweight, inexpensive wagon typically used for personal transportation. According to the Hoffays this runabout had a dark box and seat and light-colored wheels. The man sitting on the wagon had a straw hat and appeared to have a light-colored mustache. The

Hoffays could not see the man in the bushes by the pond. According to our reconstructed timeline, the Hoffays would have had to have encountered this runabout between 7:15pm and 7:25pm. However, the Hoffays did not see Hazel Drew on the road, so this implies that they passed Teal's Pond closer to 7:25pm.

Frank Smith and Rudolph Gundrum, along with Henry and Charlotte Rollman confirmed seeing the Hoffays on Taborton Road that night. However, they did not see this runabout. Between 7:25pm and 7:30pm Julia and Henry Rymiller passed Teal's Pond, traveling in the direction of Taborton, ahead of Mrs. Marie Yeabauer, traveling in the same direction. The Rymillers claimed to have encountered Frank Smith and Rudolph Gundrum, heading in the opposite direction. The *Troy Northern Budget* reported that the Ryemillers witnessed a girl on Taborton Road, however other sources stated that they did not see her. The Rymillers also did not see a wagon at Teal's Pond, as claimed by William and Elizabeth Hoffay.

DREW MURDER CLUE IN STORY AT INQUEST

Witness Huffey Tells of Strange
Men Seen Near Teal's Pond,
Where Girl Was Found.

HAZEL KILLED BY A BLOW

Autopsy Indicates Girl Was Dead Before She Was Thrown Into
the Water.

New York Times, July 28, 1908. Did the Hoffays see a mysterious runabout at Teal's Pond or were they just trying to get their hands on the reward?

Mrs. Yeabauer went on the record, reported in several sources, that she passed Teal's Pond at 7:30pm, traveling toward Taborton. She also claimed to have seen Smith and Gundrum and the Rollmans. She did not see Hazel Drew and, crucially, she did not witness the runabout which the Hoffays reported to have seen. The witnesses on the Taborton Road on that Tuesday night confirmed each other's testimony, based on their relative place-ment on the road. From this we can ascertain two key points: 1) Hazel Drew was off Taborton Road by 7:30pm and 2) the runabout seen by the Hoffays was simply not there.

Let us suppose that even if the man allegedly beating the bushes by Teal's Pond were able to get himself back into the vehicle in such a short period of time – less than five minutes - Mrs. Yeabauer would have ridden up on them, either turning back toward Sliters Corners or headed toward Taborton. According to the Hoffays the runabout was taking up a large amount of room on the road – they allegedly had to move their wagon over to allow the Hoffays to pass. For this runabout and its two passengers to have remained invisible to the other riders on the road that night would have been impossible.

The testimony required to put together this timeline was not fully available to investigators until the public inquest. At the outset the authorities took this clue seriously. In fact, they took it so seriously that they rousted a fellow out of bed the morning after the headline broke who bore a resemblance to the runabout's driver. This man's name was William J. Cushing, and we will discuss him further, momentarily.

By July 20, 1908, when the Hoffays told their tale, clues were drying up. The press and the police jumped all over the Hoffays hoping for a lead. William Hoffay was asked by the press almost immediately why he hadn't come forward sooner. He obfus-cated, stating that he and his wife simply lived far from town and hadn't heard the news. For this to be true, this means they didn't read the paper or hadn't heard any local gossip for more than a week. The pressmen were suspicious of the testimony almost immediately, chalking it up at an attempt to grab the reward. On July 21st, D.A. O'Brien dismissed the Hoffays story, stating that the two men were probably out trolling Teal's Pond for bait-fish. By July 24th, he'd dismissed the story entirely. Recall that O'Brien, throughout the investigation, reported that he had built a timeline of the case. Even without a computer database, by July 24th it would have become obvious that the Hoffays' story simply didn't fit.

O'Brien hedged saying that perhaps the Hoffays had seen the runabout a different night. That way he could acknowledge their confirmed presence on the road that night without having to outright call them liars. But some of the pressman went ahead called them liars, anyway. The inquest began a few days later on July 27th and the Hoffays' testimony was a non-story by that time.

We could easily ignore the Hoffays story, simply because the runabout's presence on the road isn't credible, were it not for the fact that subsequent researchers have taken their claim quite seriously. The authorities in 1908 made every attempt to run the lead to the ground, going to every stable and every place in the region where such a runabout could be leased. The investigators came up with virtually nothing, beyond the aforementioned Mr. Cushing.

The men seen by the Hoffays were either fictitious or misremembered from another occasion and thus, the drivers of the alleged runabout did not kill Hazel Drew.

THE POLITICIAN

William J. Cushing must have lost his mind when the cops came bursting through the door, waking him from his night's sleep, to ask questions about Hazel Drew. The case had obviously been in the papers and no doubt Mr. Cushing was in a bit of a panic to find himself connected to it. Cushing was a young man, only a few years older than Hazel Drew herself. He lived with his mother and worked in a bottling plant, for the maker of a local soft drink called "Hoxie."

Cushing was a small-time politico who'd gotten himself elected as the Republican Committeeman for Troy's Eleventh Ward. The authorities came to Cushing's door as the result of the testimony made by the Hoffays related to the runabout they claimed to have seen by Teal's Pond on the night of July 7th. In following up that clue the authorities visited every stable in the region searching for a horse and carriage that might have been leased out that night headed to Sand Lake. They turned up one—a runabout leased to Cushing by William T. Shyne's livery. Cushing was young and unmarried. He told the authorities that, yes, he *had* been out to Sand Lake with a girl on July 7, 1908 – but not Hazel Drew. Cushing stated that he had his friend, Fred Schatzle, who worked for a local undertaker, telephone Shyne to reserve a horse and carriage. This might seem suspicious at first, but remember that in 1908 most people, even in an urban area, still didn't have a telephone. The young politician then took his girl on an evening ride. He would have had to tell the livery where he was going in case something went wrong and they needed to come looking for him. Cushing made it clear, however, that though he went to Sand Lake, he did not go up Taborton Mountain and toward Teal's Pond.

William Cushing's involvement in the case came and went in the matter of a day, a dead end. Obviously Schatzle and the girl Cushing was with (whose name was not mentioned) could provide Cushing with an alibi. Cushing was mentioned in the papers on July 23, 1908. On July 24th O'Brien dismissed the Hoffays' story as unreliable.

The reason we must consider Cushing as a possible suspect is because of David Bushman and Mark T. Givens' book *Murder at Teal's Pond: Hazel Drew and the Mystery that Inspired Twin Peaks*. It is not my intention to spoil Bushman and Givens' book, but in summary they accept the Hoffays' story of seeing the runabout near Teal's Pond on the night of July 7th as factual and accurate. They then go a step further and argue that this runabout was the very same one leased by Cushing and that Cushing and Schatzle were the two men witnessed by the Hoffays.

Note that the police thought the description of one of the men, who had a moustache, matched that of Cushing. Bushman and Givens go into a lot of detail to build a conspiracy to murder Hazel Drew as the result of a hit put out on her by the local Republican establishment, an assassination carried out by Cushing and Schatzle. While I agree that Hazel was in a position to know a lot about the internal machinations of the Troy GOP, it remains very clear that she was not assassinated, as previously argued.

For Cushing to be a suspect we must accept the Hoffays' story as accurate despite all the evidence to the contrary. Second, Cushing went out riding *with a girl*, not another man. This girl could not have been Hazel Drew because Hazel was witnessed walking to Teal's Pond herself, on her own. Third, Hazel would have arrived at Teal's Pond only slightly earlier than when the Hoffays claimed to have seen the runabout. The runabout was gone by the time Mrs. Yeabauer arrived, if it were there at all. Not only would this runabout have had to have been practically invisible, Cushing and Schatzle would have had to do their killing in mere seconds, toss the body, and stage the scene in the handful of minutes between the Hoffays arrival and the arrival of others traveling up Taborton Road. The timeline simply does not work. Finally, as we've established based on the evidence of the autopsy and the finding of Hazel's nose glasses, it's clear she was not assassinated, but died from a fall. Cushing was with a girl, per his own admission, O'Brien and the pressmen need only check with her to dismiss him as a suspect (which they no doubt did).

The politician, William J. Cushing, did not kill Hazel Drew.

THE FAMILY

Hazel Drew's family were weird people—isolated, introverted, seemingly uncaring, and, as the press kept reporting, "peculiar." Hazel herself it seems, was the exact opposite of this—precocious, gregarious, fun-loving, and out-going. Hazel's mother, Julia, was disabled. As a result, she would not have been able to share the type of outgoing adventures that Hazel enjoyed with her Aunt Minnie. Minnie seemed to act as a kind of surrogate mother to Hazel and was certainly her protector.

A lot was made of the fact that Julia Drew seemed to be unemotional in various proceedings related to the case, as well as the fact that her family immediately cashed Hazel's insurance policy.

Since they were not wealthy people and needed money to make their child's funeral arrangements, this makes perfect sense. In addition, when Julia and John were allowed to talk away from the watchful eye of District Attorney O'Brien—and Aunt Minnie—they got quite emotional about their daughter, to include Julia's belief that her daughter had been hypnotized by a prominent man.

No accusation of foul play fell upon Hazel's immediate family. The entire news media assumed that Aunt Minnie was involved in a cover up, because she kept admitting as much. Regardless, O'Brien allowed Minnie to get away with this obfuscation, to the great frustration of the pressmen (and me). But no one thought she killed Hazel Drew, nor should we. However much of her family's behavior was odd and suspicious and we should be comfortable in believing they knew more than they told.

On the other hand, considerable suspicion fell upon Hazel's uncle, and Julia and Minnie's brother, William Taylor, whose farm at which she had sought refuge during her illness and to which she may have been traveling on the night of July 7, 1908. William Taylor was heavily criticized for his apparent lack of curiosity regarding the presence of his niece at his farm during her illness. When informed she might have been on the way to his house on July 7th, he did not seem to care. When a body was found, he was uncurious and did not care. When the body was identified as that of his niece, he did not go to see it. He went to Troy to sell produce from his farm. He missed the graveside service for Hazel's funeral.

There was bad blood between Uncle Will and Hazel's father John Drew, but it seemed not to have spoiled the relationship among the Drew children with their uncle. Hazel's older brother and sister-in-law were working for Taylor when Hazel took ill. News reports indicate that Taylor had respect for his niece and often deferred to her, despite her age, in matters of serious concern. In choosing to go to Taborton Mountain, after sunset, Hazel was certain that she was walking toward safety and refuge, not into danger. This was the same place she had chosen, earlier in the year, when she needed help.

If Hazel wanted to schedule a meet-up and was down to her last nickel, Teal's Pond isn't a bad meeting place. Though Hazel lived in Troy, Poestenkill and Taborton were her home turf. Her Uncle Will lived across the street from Teal's Pond, Conrad Teal's family were old and venerable and was on good terms with everyone, and Hazel's brother Willie was boarding with the Sowalskie family just a little further up the road. If we factor in the possibility that Hazel knew Dr. Knauff and/or his son, her last nickel would get her back to his country home without her having to disturb her uncle. For Hazel, Teal's Pond was both secluded and safe.

What is to be made of William Taylor's seemingly suspicious behavior? That's explained by the recent developments in the man's personal life. In 1903, Taylor lost his wife Emelia, who passed away at age 59. Going forward, Taylor fought terrible episodes of depression. It was reported he proposed marriage to the widow Sowalskie, only to be rebuffed. The culmination of this loss and sadness resulted in William Taylor attempting to take his own life by slitting his wrists.

Rather than being a callous and indifferent man, William Taylor was clearly a man of deep feeling and emotional connection, who struggled with the Black Dog well before anti-depressants were available to help. He did not, as many did, turn to drink and laudanum, but rather to his work and his farm, for distraction. The death of a favored niece, who had shared his home, would have been highly triggering for Taylor so it is likely that rather than being indifferent, he engaged in avoidance to curb a depressive spiral.

At the outset of the case, Jarvis O'Brien was openly hostile to Taylor, but by the end he portrayed the man in the media sympathetically. Taylor was dismissed by the D.A. as being morose and peculiar and not a serious suspect. Taylor did get to enjoy some happiness later in life. In 1911 he married a divorcee, Julia Miller, and resided with her until her death in 1932. Taylor then moved in with his widowed sister and Hazel's mother, Julia, and passed away in 1934 at the age of 81.

Hazel Drew was not killed by a member of her family.

THE FARM BOY

If District Attorney Jarvis O'Brien had wanted to stitch someone up to pin Hazel Drew's murder on, Frank Smith was the most likely suspect. Frank, referred to in his time as "slow," "funny," and "peculiar," was certainly what today we would refer to as being on the autism spectrum. His behavior was noted by reporters in various interactions and Smith often was unaware of his situation and clearly misread social queues. Smith appeared at Hazel's inquest sporting a clean white shirt and puffing on a big cigar, as if he were a celebrity prize fighter, rather than a witness potentially under suspicion for murder. Frank Smith clearly enjoyed attention, even when it was clear he was being made the butt of jokes. His run to the Averill Park Post Office and his antics running around a tree at Crape's Hotel on the night of Hazel's murder, are indicators that Smith probably was not always aware of the reality of his circumstances. Smith, however, obviously had a strong body and a lot of stamina. After an evening of whisky and beer, I'm lucky to be able to run to the bathroom, yet Smith was able to run all over Sliters Corners and Averill Park while still making the hard walk up Taborton Mountain to get home. Smith never married, never moved out of the Sand Lake area, worked his entire life as a hired farm hand, and died in 1970, around the age of 80. In 1950 he was living with, ironically, the Teal family as a boarder and looking for work, despite being on the verge of turning 60. A characteristic of Smith's involvement in the Hazel Drew case was the remarkable consistency of his story. D.A. O'Brien and the other authorities frequently "sweated" Smith, including during the phase of the inquest held in Averill Park. He was frequently tracked down and interviewed by the newspapermen. Smith and Rudy Gundrum encountered Hazel Drew on Taborton Road, about the area known as the Hollow, just before Taylor's Turn, near both Teal's Pond and her Uncle William Taylor's farm. Smith claimed to have said hello to Hazel and received a hello in return and he also claimed that he mentioned to Gundrum the girl was John Drew's oldest daughter. Further,

Smith claimed to have encountered Richmond at the Averill Park train station where he mentioned seeing Hazel on the Road. Smith clearly assumed she was headed to her Uncle's farm.

When Hazel's body was found, Smith never mentioned that the girl might be Hazel Drew. At the outset, he kept mum about his entire involvement in the episode until concern got the better of him and he started talking. He claimed he did not suspect the girl in the water to be Hazel Drew. This seems unlikely but sensing that the crime might be laid at his feet, this is the story Smith stuck to until the bitter end. In addition, his testimony was corroborated by the elusive Gundrum, the Richmond's, the cast of characters at Crape's Hotel, and all the folks trafficking Taborton Road the night of July 7th.

What makes Smith a leading suspect is not his motive, it's his means and opportunity. Frank Smith knew Hazel Drew and he was clearly sweet on her. While the Drews were living with William Taylor they had been neighbors of the Smiths. Frank, seventeen in 1908, was a little younger than Hazel. We know the Smiths and Drews were on good terms because they visited each other from time to time. Frank himself remarked on how much reading Hazel Drew liked to do. William Taylor testified that he knew the Drews had contact with the Smiths, stating that on one occasion Hazel and her mother visited the Smith farm to listen to the Graphophone—the brand name of a phonograph. While it's likely the acquaintance between Frank Smith and Hazel Drew was casual, it was familiar. Frank very obviously liked the girl and was excited by her presence in his neighborhood. It seems clear he was not out to kill her when he and Gundrum saw her on the road.

Late in the case, some suspicion fell on the widow Sowalskie's boy, who had a reputation for being a sadistic bruiser. He was known to be cruel to animals and had mental deficiencies similar to Frank Smith's. Though, Sowalskie never developed as a lead, he was suspect because of his reputation. On the other hand, Frank Smith was thought of as a figure of fun and a good-natured kid. Following Hazel's death, he stayed out of the papers and lived what appears to have been a quiet life. To hang the girl's murder on Smith requires a scenario like this: Hazel, perhaps feeling morose at the loss of her job and her prospects, decided to call upon her uncle for refuge as she had during her illness. Her brother was also in the area, so she could spend a little time with him. Instead of making her way directly to his farm, she decided to spend some time at Teal's Pond in quiet reflection, out of the heat, and the time simply got away from her. Smith, buzzing with beer and whisky and all the attention he had received, left Crape's Hotel between 11:00pm and midnight and, in passing Teal's Pond, caught sight of Hazel. He decided to join her and perhaps got a little too handsy, they had an altercation, he pushed her, she fell and hit her head, and in a moment of panic he gathered her things and tossed her body into the pond to cover his tracks.

With forensic science in its infancy, a good prosecutor, armed with an angry jury, could have probably made that scenario stick, and sent Frank Smith to the chair. His behavior when the body was found was, indeed, suspicious. However, there is a major flaw with that theory – early on the morning of July 8, Frank Smith went out looking for Hazel Drew. He mentioned to his mother he'd seen her on Taborton Road. He searched for her at neighboring farms as well as her uncle's house. He later told O'Brien and the pressmen that he was hoping to "call" on her. Rather than being the actions of a killer, Smith was legitimately concerned for Hazel's well-being.

Frank Smith knew that Hazel Drew was alone on Taborton Road just before sunset. He learned from the Richmonds while in Averill Park that Hazel had not gone to her uncle's farm. In addition, he would have been passing Teal's Pond just about the time Mrs. Nennstiel claimed to have heard a car in the area which the authorities never accounted for. Even today, with the road at a higher elevation and the trees and undergrowth very thick, walking along Taborton Road, one has a very clear view of Teal's Pond. The moon was out on July 7th, 1908 and we have to wonder if Smith, trotting home after his night of fun, didn't spot something at the pond that gave him cause for concern. Did he see Hazel and her killer? Did he see a strange car? Did he see the shape in the water later mistaken for a bundle of rags? Did he hear a conversation?

At the outset O'Brien had Smith hard in the frame – he was a suspect and the press played him up as the lead. However, by the time of the inquest, his affable behavior and the remarkable consistency of his story had reduced him to being just a witness, though a challenging one. Frank Smith's intellectual capacity no doubt played a role in O'Brien not pushing harder on him as a suspect. Unlike Sowalskie, he had a good reputation. Frank Smith lived the rest of his life in a community that clearly tended to him to a very ripe old age. O'Brien was never going to hang a murder on such a person on his home turf, so in the end, he didn't try.

Frank Smith may have been a crucial, untapped witness and he almost certainly knew more than he told, but he, the farm boy, did not kill Hazel Drew.

THE HUSBAND

Of all the characters in this narrative, the person who behaved with arguably the most overt suspicion was the husband of Mina Jones, Frank. Recall that Frank moved his wife and son to Providence, Rhode Island and then, following Hazel Drew's 1908 visit, to their hometown of Waterville, Maine, while he found a job back in Troy. Frank Jones boarded with the daughter of his deceased employer and, according to testimony, spent his evenings reading. However, as Mina's publicized letters to Hazel confirmed, Mina was unhappy with this situation and requested that Hazel intervene on her part and remind Frank that he had a family in another state.

Mina Jones knew more about Hazel's life than anyone outside of her family. Mina Jones cuts a tragic figure in this story, isolated from her friends in Troy and relegated to her small hometown while her husband lived and worked in a place where Mina would have clearly preferred to have been. On Hazel's first big outing on her own, after recovering from her illness and going to work for the Carys, Mina was the first pal she chose to visit. They must have talked about many things—life, relationships, and all the gossip that goes along with emotional entanglement. I have opened the door to the possibility they were more than just friends. Though that speculation might be incorrect, it's clear that Mina and Hazel were very good friends to the point that Mina felt on equal footing with her aunt in discussing Hazel's affairs.

We do not know why Frank Jones moved his wife away from Troy, while at the same time remaining there himself. Mina died not too long after Hazel from a disease related to the lungs. So, moving her to Waterville for her health makes no sense, where it was even colder and wetter than Troy. Clearly Frank wanted Mina and their son far away from Troy and on home ground, where Mina was lonely and unhappy.

What makes Frank Jones a compelling suspect is his highly suspicious behavior. Here was a man with a wife and kids back home and couch surfing with an heiress far away from his family. His wife implored one of her oldest friends to intercede on her behalf and compel her husband to come home. The very same weekend that old friend—Hazel Drew—was murdered, Frank Jones disappeared from Troy, never to return.

While the authorities were out looking for Frank, his landlady, Ms. Fuller, reported that Frank had told her that he was planning to be away in Boston that Independence Day weekend visiting friends. But Frank never returned to Troy and did, indeed reunite with his wife in Maine. If we view the Boston trip as a cover story, it's very easy to build a murder scenario around this odd behavior.

Let us suppose that Hazel, after leaving her job, decided to go ahead and make good on Mina's request to ask her husband to return home. She may have arranged that conversation to take place at Teal's Pond, out of the light of prying eyes (especially if Hazel and Mina were in any way intimate). Frank Jones, jealous and angry, may have acted out, shoved Hazel, and then tossed her body in the water to cover things up. Fearing incrimination,

Frank high-tailed it back to Troy, hopped a train, and got himself
to Waterville.

To get to this theory we face the same problem as other suspects
without access to independent transportation and which require a
lot of supposition to create motive. We know that Hazel and Mina
were great friends. It seems unlikely that Frank Jones and Hazel were
intimate. If anything, Frank may have been interested in his landlady. Frank's motive to kill Hazel is nebulous—it would have been in
a fit of anger. The question then, is, why Teal's Pond? If Hazel Drew
had wanted to confront Frank Jones there was no reason to do it in
such a remote location—his boarding house was in town. They
could have chatted at a tavern or tearoom—or at Joe Drew's house.
Or walking along the Hudson. Hazel knew the Jones; she was a guest
in their home. It would not be seen as out of the ordinary.

But let us suppose then that for whatever illogical reason, Hazel
chose to meet Frank Jones at Teal's Pond. He then took her life.
Frank would be faced with all the problems our other suspects
without means must have faced: trying to get away without
being detected. What raises suspicion regarding Frank's actions
is the rapidity with which he got the hell out of town just at the
time that Hazel was being killed.

I think this implies not that Frank was the murderer, but that he
might have *known* that Hazel was murdered. Let us allow that
Frank legitimately went to Boston for the Independence Day
weekend. Mina Jones wrote her letter to the *Troy Record* on July
13th, literally the day after Hazel's body was identified. News
traveled to Waterville, Maine fast apparently. It seems likely to
me that Aunt Minnie, in her search for Hazel, may have already
alerted the Jones' to Hazel's disappearance. If Frank were out of
town for a few days, finding out that Hazel was missing, he may
have decided to make himself permanently scarce and go home
to his wife and son directly from Boston. In fact, whether his
actions were connected to Hazel's death or not, that's clearly
what Frank Jones did. O'Brien and his men appear to have
confirmed the alibi that Frank was in Boston with friends. The
suspicion arises in that Frank simply decided to stay gone—and

this could be because he and Mina may have suspected who killed Hazel and Troy was too hot for them.

I hope we may someday learn more about the relationship between Hazel Drew and Mina Jones. Perhaps a reader of this book will be digging around in an attic in Waterville and come across a stack of yellowed letters, hidden away from Aunt Minnie. However, due to a lack of opportunity and means to carry out the killing without detection, we can safely say that the husband, Frank Jones, did not kill Hazel Drew.

[1] Herrick, Clinton B. *Railway Surgery: A Handbook on the Management of Injuries.* New York, William Wood and Company, 1899.
[2] Hughes, *Who Killed Hazel Drew?*
[3] *Northern Budget,* July 19, 1908.
[4] Hughes, *Who Killed Hazel Drew?*

THE KILLER

CHAPTER 21

If Hazel Drew was the embodiment of Troy and its ambitious working-class desire for betterment, then so was her killer, whose use of servants no doubt allowed him to see workers as property. The man was a user, caught skimming money from his public office to favor family and friends. These were scruples of the patroons and Robber Barons of the Hudson, perched in their fine homes on the Hill, gazing down at the grit and fog of the factories and mills below that churned steel and cotton into the gold that lined their pockets.

Who would miss a dead servant girl?

Who would even care?

Doubtless, like other corpses found strewn about Rensselaer County over the previous decades there wouldn't even be an investigation. But this time people did care. Maybe it was the murder of Grace Brown so recently on everyone's mind. Maybe it was Hazel's beauty and popularity. Or, hell, maybe it was Hazel's ghost visiting people in their damn dreams. But whatever it was, this time people *did* care. Even in death Hazel Drew had a power to compel, right down to the present day. From the moment the light went out in her eyes, her killer ensured that her candle would burn brightly forever.

Now, after more than a century, that killer can be revealed.

The well to do man of Troy. The man about town with the receding hairline. The hypnotist. Her latest salvation, her patron, and possibly her lover. This man, as O'Brien prescribed, would have known the area around Teal's Pond—and truthfully all the backroads of the county—like the back of his hand and been so ubiquitous as to move unnoticed. The man with the means, the motive, and the opportunity, who could be seen anywhere and nowhere without notice was *Professor Edward Richard Cary*, Hazel Drew's final employer.

Transit, Rensselaer Polytechnic Institute Yearbook, 1914.
Professor Cary as he appeared in 1914.

Who was Edward Cary? Unlike other characters in our story, he did a fairly good job of remaining out of the papers, despite being imminent in the engineering field. Edward Richard Cary was born December 19, 1865, and was a native of Troy. His parents were Tallman Cary, Jr. and Elizabeth Lounsbury Cary. Tallman, Jr. was the son of Tallman Cary, Sr., born in 1797, and though he may have been from Massachusetts he was settled in Rensselaer County by 1820. Edward Cary had one sister, Emma Cary Gormly, who lived and died in Troy. The bulk of the Cary family is buried in Oakwood Cemetery in Troy, the same resting place as Uncle Sam Wilson.

Cary graduated from Rensselaer Polytechnic Institute with what was the equivalent of a bachelor's degree in 1888 and almost immediately joined the college faculty as an assistant professor of geodesy. This is a branch of surveying, with an eye toward projecting the earth and its features in three dimensions. In 1904 Cary was made Professor of Railroad Engineering, which seems to have been his absolute passion.

Cary taught at RPI for an astounding 48 years and a perusal of college yearbooks indicate that he taught a wide range of classes in addition to surveying and railroad engineering, to include timber selection and botany. He even seems to have had an interest in aviation. Cary wrote a few articles and couple of books that were notable in their day, to include: *Solution of Railroad Problems by Use of the Slide Rule* (1913) and *Geodetic Surveying* (1916). He may have been a Freemason. He was certainly active in the American Society of Civil Engineers, the American Railway Engineering Association, the New York Railroad Club, and Tau Beta Pi, the engineering honor society, which Cary helped establish at RPI.

Professor Cary seems to have liked money and pursued it at length. Stray clues here and there show that he invested in a wide array of projects and was also a generous donor to various charities. Unlike a lot of his contemporaries in this story – for instance Jarvis P. O'Brien—Cary not only lived in Troy's finest neighborhood, he *owned* his home. Cary's house at 9 Whitman Court, where Hazel Drew lived, was built in 1906 and may have been designed by the imminent architect Marcus Cummings. The Cary home was modern, clean, and unfussy, unlike the Victorian dwelling he and his wife Mary originally settled in. Cary's own trolley line designs and water works serviced his neighborhood.

Professor Cary married Mary Lyman on June 21, 1892, following the announcement of their engagement in the local press. Their daughter Helen was born November 26, 1896. Professor Cary never seemed to have, at any given time, just one

job—he always had multiple income streams. Right out of
college he went into private civil engineering practice at his own
firm, Cary and Roemer, which he worked at until 1905. He was
the engineer for the Hoosick Falls Electric Railway, the Hoosick
Falls and Bennington Electric Railway, and the Ballston
Terminal Railway. He was a consulting engineer for the sewer
systems at Poultney, Vermont and Corning, New York. He also
worked for the Watervliet Hydraulic Company and the famous
Wynantskill Knitting Company. Cary also seems to have served
for much of his career as the City Engineer for the towns of
Watervliet and Green Island, New York. Between 1900 to 1903
and 1906 to 1908 Cary served as the City Engineer for Troy.

In 1903, according to an engineering trade publication, Cary
was forced out of the position of Troy City Engineer for "political reasons" —stated flatly he refused to take the new mayor's
orders after the Democrats took power in the city. What finally
ended Cary's career in the job was the aforementioned scandal in
his office which caused the city fathers to decree the office must
be held as an exclusive position. Despite a sizeable pay increase,
Cary felt that job wasn't worth his time and resigned.

The controversy may have stemmed from what was arguably
Edward Cary's greatest achievement as a public engineer: radical
improvements to Troy's water works. By the time Cary took up
his first post as Troy City Engineer, it had been about twenty-
five years since significant improvements were made to the Troy
water system.[1] Growth of the city was moving—or more
correctly being pushed— toward the north and then the east, in
the direction of Vermont and Massachusetts. The city fathers
were entertaining the idea of developing reservoirs among the
many rivers in the Taconic Mountains to feed Troy and its
surrounds.

In 1899 the Troy City Charter was dissolved, and the job of
water commissioner was relegated to the Commissioner of
Public Works. Troy also annexed the village of Lansingburgh to
the north of the Troy city center, which had developed its own
water supply. At that time water was already being piped to
Pawling Avenue neighborhoods, to the east of town, where the

great and the good of Troy, including Professor Cary, made their homes. As city engineer, it would now be up to Cary to unite all this hydrology into a single system.

Cary, like a lot of Trojans in his time, seems to have had a particular interest in pushing Troy to the *east* toward Bennington, Vermont along New York Highway 7, the old Hoosick Road. Such a connection would open up new land for development and sprawl, and that could make speculators a lot of money. The industrial and commercial districts of Troy sits directly at the base of the Hill, which prevents easy and direct access toward the east of the city. The annexation of Lansingburgh to the north of the central city, allowed for the creation of a more level passageway around the Hill. Sprawl had been evolving naturally up and down the Hudson and to the West. By 1900 Trojans were looking *east*, to connect their urban areas to the somewhat isolated communities in far western Vermont and Massachusetts. Cary himself settled in the "new" eastern part of Troy and his work for the electric railways was focused on development in that direction.

This may have been a dream shared by another Trojan who lived a few blocks from the Carys, a certain attorney named Jarvis P. O'Brien. Like Cary, O'Brien's work as a public official was not his main job, but a sideline. O'Brien was an attorney for the Boston and Maine Railroad, which primarily served the areas of Massachusetts, Vermont, New Hampshire, and Maine. This mighty line had one spur that originated in Troy which carried the rider east and linked Troy to Boston and all points in between, passing through Hoosick, New York, via the newly annexed village of Lansingburgh. This line was constructed as the Troy and Boston Railroad between 1848 and 1852. It became the Fitchburg Railroad in 1887 and was acquired by O'Brien's concern, the B&M in 1900.

At the same time attorney O'Brien was doing deals to link the Fitchburg to the mighty network of the B&M, Cary was at work providing water and electric train service, paralleling the B&M's eastward line, to connect the patchwork of communities between Troy and the Vermont border to that main railroad artery. Cary and O'Brien were not only both railroad men, they were both railroad men with the same agenda—who would eventually reside in the same neighborhood.

We know from the public records that Edward Cary and Jarvis O'Brien regularly crossed paths in their business dealings. On October 4, 1906, a train accident on the B&M line at the Lansingburgh station killed and injured several passengers when a military troop transport slammed at high speed into a parked passenger train waiting to enter the station. State investigators determined that to prevent this tragedy from happening again, the B&M should construct a double track along its entire spur leading to Troy, to be built at grade through the various communities through which it passed. Jarvis O'Brien represented the B&M in these proceedings, before the investigators, the courts, and the legislature and Professor Cary represented the City of Troy. All parties shared the same interest: more rail lines, better rail lines, and paid for by the taxpayers.

Much of what Cary built still stands, largely unnoticed by Trojans. The citizens of Collar City walk on his streets, live in his houses, and swim in his lakes every day. Professor Richard E. Cary served RPI and his community (and himself) for almost half a century and, as such, his college eventually named a building after him. For such an influential Trojan, Cary did not die in the city of his birth. Toward the end of his career, around the age of 70, he and his wife moved to Columbia, South Carolina, where they settled in a luxury apartment complex reminiscent in design of their home on Whitman Court. Their daughter married a man local to that city and perhaps they moved there to join her. Cary himself was already active with South Carolina railroads. Professor Cary died on July 17, 1941, of colon cancer and his wife Mary died on October 23, 1948, of pneumonia. They are buried in South Carolina rather than with their forebears and immediate family in Troy.

[1] Troy, City Corporation of. *Two Centuries of Public Service: History of the Troy Water Works.* Troy, N.Y., City of Troy, 1977.

THE KILLER IS IN THE
HOUSE
CHAPTER 22

E very true crime aficionado and every police officer knows
that the immediate suspicion in a homicide falls on the
denizens of the victim's home and their friends and
family. This is confirmed by hard data. Around the world, across
populations, depending on how the data is compiled, between
64% and 80% of women are killed by intimate partners or family
relations.[1] The FBI has consistently confirmed this same
pattern, for as long as they have collected homicide data., first
revealed via statistical analysis in the 1980's, when crime rates
were more akin to what there were in 1908 than they are today.
[2] This places Professor Cary at the top of the suspect list, as the
sole male in Hazel Drew's home.

Exploitation of domestic help was common-place in 1908
and affairs between "master and servant" was the regular stuff of
newspaper columns and popular literature. When Hazel died
Professor Cary was 42 years old. He was a wiry, well-dressed and
tight-skinned man who, throughout his life, looked far less than
his years. The press had no problem asking Dr. Knauf, who was
49 years old, if he were having an affair with Hazel Drew, but not
her employer, Professor Cary. Based on the most minimalistic
profile, Professor Cary should have been a prime suspect, at least
until an alibi could have been confirmed and the case against

him ruled out. The media chased the most outrageous leads, but not this obvious one. But of course Prof. Cary was a member of the local GOP establishment and a likely associate of the D.A.

THE MYSTERY CAR

One of the most difficult questions that has arisen over the course of this investigation regards how the murderer arrived and departed from the scene without being detected. Whether you favor C.E.S. or Frank Jones or Pullman Man Magner as your suspect, getting him to and from Teal's Pond late at night on July 7th is a difficult task. We know, however, that Hazel's killer arrived and departed in an automobile. We know this because tire tracks leading down to the edge of the pond were found by Gilbert Miller and the person who saw this mystery car reported it to the press.

The *Evening Star* of Newark, New Jersey reported Miller's discovery of the tire tracks, a clue unnoticed by most modern investigators and barely carried in any other outlet. The paper states: "A search of the woods revealed the tracks of the automobile, which had left the road to cut through the woods to the edge of the pond."

The car that arrived at Teal's Pond was witnessed by Mrs. Louisa Nennstiel. This clue is barely mentioned in any of the press accounts including the local Troy papers. The *Evening Star* reports that Nennstiel "said she heard the automobile at midnight on July 7 pass in front of her house and return a short time later as if bound for the Glass Lake road."[3]

According to census records, the Nennstiels were the next house up from William Taylor on the Taborton Road. They were also neighbors of Frank Smith's family. The location of Louisa's residence put her in a prime spot to see this late running auto. Coupled to Gilbert Miller spying tire tracks leading to the pond after finding Hazel's body, we can safely conclude that Hazel's killer arrived and departed in a car – a car which had to have been driven by the type of driver unafraid to take his automobile off main roads.

District Attorney O'Brien did not follow up on this clue. The pressmen, on the other hand, recognized this clue as pointing toward a killer with money enough to afford a car in the era before Henry Ford introduced his economical Model-T. However, they sought to connect it to the rumors related to Henry Kamrath's camp at Alps. When that story fell apart, so did the linkage between Hazel's killer and a car.

O'Brien himself arrived on the scene before onlookers stomped all over it, wrecking any potential clues in the landscape. If Miller saw the tire tracks, so did O'Brien. This would have *immediately* told Jarvis O'Brien that his killer was a man of wealth and privilege and that his suspect pool was small. Did he dive in trying to track down automobile owners? No. Rather, O'Brien reported to the press that he didn't believe a car could get up Taborton Mountain and that even if it could, it'd take a skillful driver to navigate such a road.

Yes. A skillful driver like the former Troy City Engineer and the present engineer of Green Island. Professor Edward Cary's business was surveying – his literal expertise for half a century. Surveyors spend their days lugging equipment into rough country. They're accustomed to navigating muddy roads and wild terrain under all kinds of conditions. Cary would be exactly the type of man—and perhaps one of the few men in the county in 1908—with the knowledge and skills to navigate Taborton Road at night.

Through careful research we know that Cary was familiar with areas around Taborton Mountian. As part of his public works duties, he had been working on the nearby Quackenkill diversion dam as early as 1900. Records of engineering projects by RPI alums indicate that he designed the concrete dam at Wynatskill in Sand Lake. To construct such a dam would have required extensive collection of surveying and hydrological data. Professor Cary knew the area because his engineering projects had taken him to the region throughout his career.

Is there any evidence that Cary owned an automobile at the time Hazel died? Besides being necessitated by his work, Cary's house at 9 Whitman Court gives us a clue. Constructed in 1906, the house was built with a matching garage, offset with a lovely driveway. He built his home and set it on his lot to accommodate a garage for a car. Which makes sense for a man of his business – he needed to get out in the field and like railroad man O'Brien, almost certainly owned an automobile in 1908.

From the moment Jarvis O'Brien saw those tire tracks he would have known that his killer was a man of his own socio-economic class. With so few cars on the road and himself an automobilist he may have even had a few guesses as to who that car belonged to. With tire tracks in hand, solving the crime should have been a simple process of elimination: which suspect had a car and among those which suspect's tire tracks matched those found at Teal's Pond? Case closed.

But O'Brien didn't take that approach. He messed around for twenty days ultimately trying to chalk the thing up to suicide at Hazel's inquest. Hazel Drew's killer arrived and departed in an automobile. Professor Cary had an automobile and on top of that the skills to pilot it off road and the knowledge of the county byways to move in and out largely unseen.

Someone should have checked his tires.

THE DEATH AND THE DISMISSAL
CANNOT BE A COINCIDENCE

It stretches credulity to believe that Hazel Drew's departure from the Cary residence and her murder are unconnected. The story that District Attorney O'Brien seemed to be pushing was that Hazel had become despondent over her direction in life and killed herself as a result. Will Clemens, on the other hand, speculated that Hazel was planning to run off with a lover and he murdered her.

I believe, however, that Hazel departed the Cary residence and made arrangements to remove herself from their home permanently. She met with her aunt and outlined her plan, which her aunt then misrepresented to the press and the investigators. She then planned to have a clandestine meeting with the person who would eventually murder her—whom she trusted—

on familiar ground, near her uncle's home, to avoid suspicion or scandal among her own friends and family and that of her killer. Perhaps she used the newspaper ad to summon her killer to Teal's Pond or perhaps he used it to summon her.

No matter how the plan was set, Hazel then had to waste time waiting for this meeting to happen, and seeking to avoid pressing questions, she spent a little time and her last few dollars on a fast overnight trip to New York City via the steamship *Saratoga* and then on the train back to Troy. This would have cost the same as a decent hotel room but not required a chaperon or the inconvenience of running into someone who could ask too many questions.

Hazel then spent the day of July 7th making her way, slowly, to Teal's Pond, without spending any other money or seeing relatives, but still being witnessed wandering around Troy. By the evening, she was making her way up Taborton Road, down to her last nickel, but fully expecting to be able to go to her uncle's house for food and a ride home or to reach some arrangement with the person whom she was meeting at the pond.

By 7:30pm Hazel took a turn to the right walking up Taborton Road, opposite the direction of Taylor's Turn and her uncle's home and made her way down to Teal's Pond through the less steep path. Hazel removed her gloves and put them down with her hat and got comfortable. There, under a partial moon, she sat to await her meeting, perhaps sitting on the very stone that would soon take her life.

Late into the evening, around midnight, at a time when he would not otherwise be noticed, the would-be killer arrived, having been witnessed by Mrs. Nennstiel. The duo had a conversation that turned into an argument. In the heat of this argument, Hazel's would-be killer lashed out and shoved her and unable to right herself, fell back and hit her head on one of the many rocks scattered about the pond. Her glasses fell to the side and disappeared into the darkened landscape. Panicked her killer decided to try to cover things up instead of running to Crape's Hotel for help, and gathered up Hazel Drew's body and tossed it into Teal's Pond.

Around about this same time a tipsy and jolly Frank Smith was making his way up Taborton Road toward home and may have seen headlights, heard raised voices, or witnessed something else to raise his suspicions. If a car were parked by the pond, he almost certainly would have seen it. The killer would quickly be starting his automobile and making his way home or back to the place from which he came. With no campers in the area that night and farmer Teal likely long asleep, little else was heard.

Hazel Drew's contact with her would-be killer must have been triggered by her departure from the Cary home. Mrs. Cary stated on several occasions that she asked Hazel, early in the morning of July 6th if she'd like to do some laundry. Instead of doing laundry, as requested, she went upstairs, packed her things, and left the house by 10:00am. This has become part of the "legend" of Hazel's demise. The request to do laundry triggered her resigning from her job which then led to her murder.

To employ a pun, the laundry story simply does not wash. It was oft repeated in the press that Hazel worked as a governess. That is someone who takes care of children. So perhaps Hazel was a domestic who performed varied tasks. But doing laundry seems unlikely. July 6, 1908, was unseasonably hot. There were plenty of laundries in Troy, with pick up and drop off services. There were even a few of these in the Cary's immediate neighborhood. It seems odd that Mrs. Cary would inflict this task on Hazel on a Monday morning, especially considering Hazel had an appointment to see Carrie Weaver off at Union Station that morning. It's even odder that Mrs. Cary would want to heat her own house up with a bunch of hot clothes. Laundry in this context would have been punishment, not a casual task.

Mrs. Cary was not interviewed extensively by the press, nor does it appear that she testified at Hazel's inquest. This is odd as she was the person who spent the most time with the girl in the last months of her life and would have known the most about her. What little Mrs. Cary did say, gives us pause for thought. At one point she told the press that Hazel didn't spend much time with people her own age. Additionally, she stated that the Carys tried to make Hazel happy. These are odd statements. Who was it Hazel preferred spending time with that wasn't her own age, as her friend group certainly consisted of young people? Aunt Minnie perhaps? Or possibly someone else?

I believe, as I have stated earlier, that the discrepancy between the various stories related to Aunt Minnie and Hazel's return to Pawling Avenue and Whitman Court on the night of July 5th gives us insight into *something* that happened which led to Hazel's departure from the home. Recall that Aunt Minnie stated that she and Hazel initially went to her abode at the Harrison house together, at which point Minnie got her clothes out of Hazel's suitcase. However, Roy Beauchamp, the conductor of the trolley that dropped them off at their respective stops swore at the inquest that they departed separately to go directly to their respective homes. If Hazel did have clothes belonging to Minnie in her case, she did not return them the night of July 6th and would have had to do so on the morning of July 7th.

Recall also that initially Professor Cary stated that Hazel had returned to his home at a good hour, but then later testified that Hazel had arrived after he had gone to bed. Beauchamp, a man whose job required him to keep a timely schedule, testified that Hazel and Minnie were dropped off between 10:30pm and 11:00pm on Sunday evening, which is late. Professor Cary's latter testimony seems to be an attempt to remove himself from having any contact with Hazel that night, to avoid potential further questions.

It seems likely, however, that *something* occurred between 11:00pm Sunday night and 10:00am Monday morning that caused Hazel to depart the Cary home. Did the two have a fight? Did they get caught by Mrs. Cary smooching or otherwise being overly intimate? Or did Professor Cary try something which Hazel wasn't ready for which discouraged her and made her want to leave? We will explore some of these possibilities. But we know through her relationship with Mrs. Tupper that Hazel was the kind of person who made friends with her employers.

These inconsistencies are suspicious. Mrs. Cary claimed that Hazel never notified her of her change of plans to skip going to

Lake George and instead go to Schenectady for the weekend. When confronted by this information, Mrs. Cary was surprised. This makes it clear that if Mrs. Cary did indeed ask Hazel to do laundry, she made no further effort to ask the girl if she'd had an enjoyable weekend. In addition, the story Mrs. Cary told was itself inconsistent. She stated she asked Hazel to do laundry around 9:00am and that the girl was out the door by 10:00am. Yet soon after first telling this tale to the police and press, that box of torn up correspondence and photos was found in the Cary basement. It seems highly unlikely Hazel could accomplish that task as well as pack her things to leave in an hour.

Mrs. Cary reported that the comb and washcloth found in Hazel's suitcase belonged to her, Mrs. Cary. This really stands out to me as a potential clue that something happened to force Hazel from the Cary home. How did those items get into Hazel's case? Hazel may have had them as part of the kit in her room and took them with her on her trip and simply did not unpack before leaving. Or she unpacked to start her week's work, and tossed it all back into her suitcase, perfectly happy to steal these items from Mrs. Cary. Finally, it's possible these items were not Mrs. Cary's, but Professor Cary's and they became co-mingled into Hazel's things during an illicit weekend trip. To me it seems likely that whatever happened Sunday night prompted Hazel to simply not unpack at all, and rather, spend the evening packing up to leave along with purging her trunk of the letters found in the basement. The laundry story was a cover to throw suspicion off the Carys.

Hazel's friends indicated that she had expressed no plans to quit the Cary's employment. This is confirmed by Carrie Weaver, who Hazel was planning to meet at Union Station on the morning of July 6th. Hazel failed to show at that *bon voyage*, but her plan to meet Carrie further rules out the laundry story. I suspect, in fact, that Hazel's morning trip to Albany, after leaving the Cary home, was an attempt to catch up to Carrie Weaver to bid her farewell. Recall that the Troy line was a spur that went to Boston and Montreal. Carrie would have likely gone to Albany and then waited on a train to take her west.

Whatever triggered Hazel's departure must have been on the night of her return to the Cary home on July 5th. Her decision to leave must have given her time to sort her things, clear out her correspondence, and dump these materials for burning in the basement. The "laundry story" seems like a concoction to explain Hazel Drew's departure after it was revealed that Hazel was dead. Hazel either decided to leave or Mrs. Cary simply fired the girl, over whatever happened the night before, once her husband was absent from the house.

If Professor Cary were absent from the home on Monday morning, as it appears he was, this would explain why Hazel would want to meet him up for a discussion, attempt at reconciliation, or more likely to make a request for money. The inconsistencies in Minnie and Professor Cary's stories force us to consider that the trigger for Hazel's departure, and ultimately her murder, were events that transpired after the return from Schenectady.

HAZEL AND THE PROFESSOR?

A consistent part of the Legend of Hazel Drew and, indeed, the part of the legend that perhaps most strongly influenced the character of Laura Palmer is the intimation that she led a double life. A domestic by day, Hazel, after her demise, became known for living a good life of expensive clothes, trips, and parties enjoyed by someone without the funds from her job to really be able to afford that lifestyle. While I think it is well-established that Hazel did like a good time and, as was the case with Mr. Magner, was certainly willing to hit up a strange man to get it, Hazel was not doing sex work.

It's clear from the fact that in her last days Hazel had to borrow money to pay her dress maker and that when she was found she was literally down to her last nickel, that Hazel spent every bit of money that came into her hands. She was smart enough to be making the payments on an insurance policy, but no other funds were ever found among her things, she was indebted to her mother, and there was no record of any kind of savings account having existed in her name. Hazel clearly relied on the room and board provided by her position to carry her through until pay day while spending her money on herself.

Hazel's trips to New York, Providence, and Boston were treated as a curiosity by the press and by subsequent investigators. The speculation is that Hazel was off meeting men. However, we know from the reports in the Providence press that letters in Hazel's trunk from these cities were from physicians. Hazel was visiting doctors.

Mrs. Cary told the press that when Hazel returned from her travels she was happy but secretive. Did the Carys give her leave to travel while they handled her duties? Or did Hazel hit the road any time the Cary's themselves were on a trip? The latter seems most likely. But there is also a third possibility: that Hazel traveled with the Carys or with Professor Cary alone on some of these voyages.

It is difficult to comprehend Hazel Drew riding the rails in 1908 completely unaccompanied. She went to New York City on Decoration Day with Carrie Weaver and traveled to Boston with Mina Jones. It is difficult to fix the timeline of Hazel's travels. Mrs. Cary asserted that Hazel took multiple trips, but it appears certain she took one long trip around the end of April 1908, which took her to New York City, Boston, and Providence. We know this was more than a long weekend because Hazel mailed her last postcard to William C. Hogardt from Providence on April 22nd, a Wednesday.

The understanding that Hazel was visiting medical men changes the narrative. Rather than having a good time, Hazel was also traveling to seek advice for her health. This makes it even more likely that she would require a chaperone, especially one of some stature.

In a tantalizing coincidence, the New York Railroad Club, according to their extant minutes, held their monthly meeting at 29 West 39th Street in New York City on the preceding Friday April 17th, beginning at 8:30pm. Professor Cary was an active member of this society and did occasionally attend their meetings. Members were required to present a card at these meetings to demonstrate their membership and their attendance was logged into the minutes. Professor Cary did not attend this April 17th meeting.

However, it seems perfectly likely that Professor Cary may have used the pretense of a meeting with his club to chaperone Hazel on the first leg of her journey. Indeed, such an arrangement would have not only been appropriate, but *more appropriate* than Hazel traveling alone. This would have given the duo time to do...other things. It's clear Hazel didn't mind changing plans or even lying about her intentions, as was the case with the YWCA stay.

Is there any evidence that Hazel Drew and Professor Cary were even seen in each other's company? Professor Cary was not the type of man to advertise his whereabouts in the social columns. His comings and goings were not reported, as was often the custom among the high society types at the time. Except with regard to his official business, he kept his name out of the papers. Obviously, the clincher clue would be to find a report of Hazel and the Professor, together, in a place such as New York City where they were not supposed to be. Maybe that clue is out there, and we will find it.

Until such time there is one intriguing piece of circumstantial evidence. In the earliest hours of the investigation, when attempts were being made to track down any and all of Hazel's associates there was a search going on for a man whom Hazel had been seen with who had "a very marked cast of features." This man had a long nose and a "receding forehead."[4] He was balding. The paper itself pointed out that no such person matching that description had ever come to light until Peter Cipperly claimed to see such a man in the company of a girl who looked like Hazel Drew on the Albia Car headed toward Sand Lake. As the paper states, "no trace of such a person could be found." *Except that is not true.* This description perfectly describes Hazel Drew's boss, Edward Cary.

There are photos available of Professor Cary both at the archives of Rensselaer Polytechnic Institute and in their yearbooks published during his career that are available on-line. The

Professor was beginning to bald at the time of his graduation in 1888. By 1908 his receding hairline had reached the midpoint of his head. He did, in fact, have quite a prominent nose. He also sported a mustache.

The *only person* in Hazel Drew's life with this set of features was Professor Cary. Hazel Drew had been witnessed around Troy with a person who met his description. One of the interesting facts to note is that in 1908, the Engineering Building, containing Professor Cary's office, was located right at the top of The Hill on the RPI campus, atop a massive flight of stairs called the Approach.

This staircase provided easy—if exhausting—access to the town from the campus, and vice versa. At the foot of the Approach, immediately across the street was Troy Union Station. Had Hazel ever wanted to meet up with the Professor in town without being conspicuous on campus, his office was literally a flight of stairs away from the train station. It was at this same station to which Hazel kept wandering on the last two days of her life. All the spots where she was seen on those days were no more than a five-minute climb from the Professor's office. It seems entirely possible that if Hazel were attempting to liaise with Professor Cary after she left his home, these places would have been the logical spots to try to bump into him.

Professor E.R. Cary was a fascinating person. He had an interest in technology and in machines. Hazel Drew loved to read, and he most certainly had a first-class home library which. Whether he accompanied her or not, he allowed Hazel to broaden her horizons through travel. Cary was active in his church and the larger diocese, pastimes which Hazel herself had a passion for. As we will soon explore, he may have had some more fringe ideas which might have fascinated the young woman. His yearbook photos show him to be handsome, though balding, and perhaps key, extremely well-dressed. Though he was older than Hazel by a factor of two, he was her youngest employer.

Rockstar professors are charismatic and compelling people. Hazel probably liked her new boss. After moving to

Whitman Court, her life almost certainly got a lot more interesting. She was now living in the home of a professor, rather than farmers, stodgy money men, and coal sellers. The house was new, as well. There was a car parked outside and the trolley line ran at the foot of the street. Everything around Whitman Court was new and beautiful.

Hazel Drew's trips began after she began work with the Carys. Her taste in nicer clothes may have also begun at this time, as the things she had made by Mrs. Schumacher seemed to be new. In fact, she still owed money on some of her wardrobe the night she bought the shirtwaist she planned to wear to Lake George. As we know from Hazel's declining penchant for correspondence following her move to Whitman Court, in the months approaching her death she was drastically shrinking her friendship circle. In the end she truly was spending her time almost exclusively with older people: the Carys, Aunt Minnie (who lived nearby on Pawling Avenue), and through correspondence and trips, Mina Jones.

That brings us to that ill-fated weekend planned for Lake George. According to Carrie Weaver, Hazel first mentioned her intention to go to Lake George during their Decoration Day (Memorial Day) trip to NYC. Hazel had told her family that's where she was planning to go and that's also where she told Mrs. Cary she was headed, to the point Mrs. Cary still believed this was her destination at the time Hazel was killed. Hazel had just a little over a month to plan that trip, but at the very last minute, even when she did not fully have the proper funds to support it, she was up late at night demanding her dress maker create for her a new piece of finery. Hazel then got this expensive piece of clothing only to allow her aunt to talk her out of the much-anticipated travel plans at the last minute.

Let us suppose that Hazel Drew planned to go to Lake George right down to almost the last moment but then some *event* took place that would greatly enhance her weekend. Maybe an opportunity to have a more interesting companion at Lake George - or somewhere equally interesting—presented itself. To be in the company of this new companion and not be so obviously a member of the lower classes, Hazel would need to look good—better than she was planning to look in the company of her aunt and better than she'd looked when she went to NYC with Carrie. Suddenly nothing in her trunk would do for this weekend outing. After getting off work on Friday evening, she made a fast trip to the Boston Store for fabric and then turned up at Mrs. Schumacher's front door begging for the work to be done.

But what kind of event could have changed Hazel's plans so drastically at the last minute? Possibly a tragedy.

On Saturday June 29, 1908—a week before Hazel Drew had planned to visit the town—a trio of wealthy revelers consisting of William Sidney Nicholson, his wife, his Mother-in-law, Mrs. R.A. Mosher, and a Miss Louise Brown climbed into Nicholson's touring car and began making their way back to their residence in Albany from a day trip to the Sagamore Resort. As they approached the town of Halfmoon, no doubt with a drink or two in them, around 8:45pm, (after dark) they ran up on a farmer who was driving a team of horses through a narrow stretch of road bordered by ditches. To avoid a collision, Nicholson swerved his automobile to the right, but caught a tire at the edge of a ditch and flipped the vehicle.

The women in the party were thrown free of the wreck and, though injured, survived. Mr. Nicholson was not so lucky. As the car flipped, it struck him in the back of the head and broke his neck, killing him instantly. Mr. Nicholson was the Superintendent of the Hudson River Telephone Company, so the story received extensive media coverage. His death also led to an investigation and liability litigation that went all the way to the New York Supreme Court. It is from that litigation that we obtain a very important clue. Mrs. Nicholson filed suit against the town of Stillwater, New York, which had jurisdiction over road maintenance at the site of the accident. The suit alleged that the roads were not safe and suitable for passing traffic.

To assess the situation, shortly after the accident, an expert surveyor and engineer was called for: Professor E.R. Cary. Cary would go on to testify for the Plaintiff, Mrs. Nicholson, in her various court proceedings, which lasted until 1912. We do not know when Cary was called into the case, but it's clear he was brought on board quickly. During the 1912 New York Supreme Court hearing, Cary stated that he took a series of measurements on July 9, 1908, from which he made a map of the accident scene. As you will recall, this is only two days after Hazel Drew was murdered on July 7th.

The Nicholson accident occurred on June 29th. Professor Cary is confirmed, by his own admission, to have been onsite on July 9th. It is not hard to speculate that the City Engineer of Green Island would have been called into the case very early, possibly by the coroner, as Green Island was certainly the closest municipality with a significant engineering program.

If we can imagine Hazel and the Professor enjoying his work trips as a means of spending time together then it is not impossible to imagine a scenario in which Cary proposed that he horn his way into her Lake George trip under the pretense of investigating the Nicholson death. If Hazel Drew did travel to Schenectady on Saturday evening, she would have been about 15-16 miles to the east and south of the crash site. In addition, the railroad line that runs immediately adjacent to the crash site led directly to the main station at Schenectady. It would have been no effort at all for Hazel Drew to have rendezvoused with Professor Cary at some rural station between her cousin's house and the accident site either Saturday evening, when we know she left Troy, or on Sunday morning.

We can imagine this conversation between Edward and Mary Cary: "You know since it's the holiday weekend, I believe I will skip the services and drive the route driven by that poor Mr. Nicholson up to the Sagamore to get a feeling for the traffic and conditions on before I go out this week and take my measurements. Maybe I'll run into Hazel and that aunt of hers! Don't wait up for me." Plans set for a grand day out.

DREW CASE BAFFLES TROY AUTHORITIES

Unable to Find Out Where Girl
Passed Night Before She
Was Murdered.

THEORY. OF AUTO ACCIDENT

Police Investigating Trips Which Girl
Made to New York, Boston,
and   Providence.

*New York Times July 17, 1908. The press frequently reported
that the investigators were "baffled," with Jarvis O'Brien
sticking to his suicide theory and others claiming Hazel was
hit by a car and dumped. Was this legitimate confusion or
evidence of a cover-up?*

A trip to the Sagamore would account for fancy dress rather than the surveyor's coveralls he would be wearing while in the field. (Obviously one would not go to such a famous spot without popping in for a drink and a meal). The coincidence of Lake George and the last-minute need for nice clothes is too compelling not to allow for speculation. The Sagamore—or one of the elite hotels in Schenectady, such as the Edison—would explain the need for the very fancy shirtwaist Hazel suddenly needed.

Cary would have returned home in his automobile while allowing Hazel and Minnie to reconvene and ride their trollies home – no one the wiser. Though perhaps over a drink that night, Mrs. Cary heard the duo reminiscing over the day. Queue Hazel Drew's exit from the Cary home, without the need for a particularly deep or nefarious affair. This would also explain Professor Cary's need to change his story and Mrs. Cary's genuine surprise at the fact that Hazel had made her way to Schenectady, because Mary Cary knew Hazel was in Lake George and wasn't aware of the cover story.

It's an elegant theory. I admit it's a theory, one which relies on the bizarre coincidence of the Nicholson accident and Professor's Cary's involvement. We know Cary was home on Sunday night. We know he was at the accident site, for sure, on July 9th.

We do not know where he was on July 6th and 7th. Did he decide to make his base at the scene of the accident? If he did, I have established that it was possible to drive from that site to Teal's Pond, using roads extant in 1908, without the need to pass through either Troy, Sand Lake, or Averill Park, coming in from the north. This would fit with Mrs. Neenstiel's witnessing a car headed from and toward the Glass Lake Road. If Cary left his home at Whitman Court to go to Teal's Pond on the night of July 7th, that drive would have been even easier, bringing him in from that same direction. Coming in from Whitman Court he would not even have needed to refuel as that drive is less than six miles.

According to an article on RPI courses published in the July 8, 1908, *Troy Record* Professor Cary had his July to himself. He planned to teach a practical railroad surveying class from the field in August 1908. But the July course was in electrical engineering and taught by Professor Green, Carrie Weaver's boss. Cary would have time to come and go as he pleased under the guise of working on the Nicholson case – or any number of his other enterprises. The man wasn't expected to be in a classroom at the time Hazel Drew was killed.

THE HYPNOTIST

There is one more "coincidence" I want to present that brings the Professor even tighter into the frame. However, I struggle with just how on the nose it is. Ewing Virgil Neal was among the most unlikely American millionaires and a man of some notoriety during Hazel Drew's lifetime. You've never heard of the guy, but what's important is that *I have.* Neal was a business lecturer, author, publisher, maker and seller of patent medicines and cosmetics, and, *above all else, a hypnotist.* He tried several angles to make his fortune, from teaching to publishing to professional stage hypnotist, finally settling on mail order medicines and cosmetics. It was the latter career that made him his fortune, allowing him to buy fancy cars and, when the law started to get on his tail, fine homes in Europe.

Neal was not, however, Hazel Drew's killer, nor even a suspect. One of Neal's many hustles was running a correspondence school called The New York Institute of Science, which he ran under the absurd pseudonym of Xenophon LaMotte Sage and claiming multiple advanced university degrees. Under this fancy stage name, he and his wife traveled around the country performing feats of mesmerism and trying to sell people on the art of personal magnetism and hypnotic control.

Neal was a prolific writer, even authoring a couple of legitimate texts on accounting principles. Around 1900 he issued the book *The Philosophy of Personal Influence*. The book provides a general outline of the principles of hypnotism and functions as an advertisement for the Xenophon LaMotte Sage correspondence courses on developing the power. In keeping with such advertising publications of the era, the pamphlet is chock-full of personal testimonials from everyone from Ivy League school administrators to medical practitioners to traveling salesmen. For instance, a dentist claimed hypnotism allowed him to perform dental surgery without anesthetic. Salesmen claimed their skills at magnetism allowed them to convince their prospects to make a buy. On and on, page after page.

On page 52 of the document is one such set of testimonials entitled "Dr. Sage before Clubs and Educational Institutions." It reads: "This is to state that Dr X. La Motte Sage has given us a highly interesting and successful demonstration of the remarkable power of hypnotism, using as subjects parties who volunteered from among those present, all of them residents of our city and known to us." Along with a number of schools and clubs ranging from Franklin-Marshall College to the Maryland Bicycle Club, Rensselaer Polytechnic Institute is represented as a signatory. The representative from RPI signing this testimonial was not one of the campus' philosophers, psychologists, or metaphysicians, but a certain engineering faculty member named E.R. Car[e]y.[5]

Hazel Drew's mother told the *New York Times* her theory of Hazel's killer: "I believe it was some one [sic] who was well to do, and who had Hazel in his control, who took her out to Averill

Park. He hypnotized my Hazel and she did whatever he asked of her. He took her out there while she was under his influence and murdered her."

District Attorney Jarvis O'Brien acted immediately to shut this theory down, informing the press that this idea was "absurd." He even went so far as to deny that the interview ever happened, stating that Mrs. Drew was "careful" with her statements. What is absurd is the idea that Hazel's family had no clue as to the identity of her killer. In fact, I think that if they didn't know outright, they certainly had a strong suspicion. It is hard to believe that Aunt Minnie didn't know, playing on her silence to protect herself and her family.

Professor Cary had a wide array of interests, electricity, electric trains, and aviation. In the early 1900s these were fringe ideas and bleeding edge concepts, akin to Quantum Computing and advances in Artificial Intelligence today. The same was true, in 1900, of hypnotism, which has only in recent decades become discredited. It fits that a man who trafficked in "crazy ideas" like airplane travel might find the concept of hypnotism appealing and interesting. Here we have proof that Cary not only went to one of "Doctor" Sage's performances but went so far as to put his support for the concepts presented in writing, with the backing of his academic institution.

I was only way able to find this clue because I have spent decades studying mysteries, the paranormal, spiritual movements, and New York's burned over district. In trying to discover if they were any validity to Mrs. Drew's claims about a "hypnotist" I went to the potential sources of a connection, and, sure enough, stumbled upon this link between one of the era's most famous hypnotists and the man who would become my suspect. If this is a coincidence, it stretches credulity. The fact that O'Brien, who outwardly was entertaining all kinds of leads, shut this one down so fast, causes us to take this connection more seriously.

Did E.R. Cary sit Hazel down and hypnotize her? I don't know. Did he talk about hypnotism, airplanes, and electric trains at the dinner table? Almost certainly. Were Hazel Drew captivated and crushing on her boss, she would certainly tell her aunt and mother about all these wild things. Also, Cary himself would likely share that dinner table with associates like Jarvis O'Brien, speaking about these same topics with the passion typical of academics. Just as Hazel's mother described, we have a prime suspect – the man in Hazel's home – who was well to do and who had a documented interest in hypnotism. In building a circumstantial case, this clue cannot be ignored.

THE MOVING GRAVE

Hazel Drew was laid to rest on the afternoon of July 14, 1908, in what is today called the Brookside Cemetery along Plank Road across the highway from the Barberville Falls. This is in the approximate vicinity of where Hazel was born, near Blue Factory Road, and where she lived her early life. Very few people attended the service at the grave, including her uncle, Will Taylor, in large part it seems because the site of the burial was changed by Hazel's family *the very day of the funeral*.

It was initially planned that Hazel would be buried in her family plot at Mount Ida Cemetery in Troy. This location would have been more convenient for family living in Troy who wished to visit Hazel. The street cars ran nearby and Aunt Minnie, who at the time worked at the Harrison House, was literally across the street from the burial site.

However, in addition to Aunt Minnie being nearby so was Professor Cary, who resided at 9 Whitman Court, almost in site of the two Mount Ida cemeteries, old and new. I believe that members of Hazel's family may have known her killer—or at least had a very strong suspicion. This is certainly true of Aunt Minnie, who was almost certainly the last family member to see Hazel alive and who knew the full details of what transpired over her last weekend.

To be blunt, I believe Aunt Minnie knew that Cary killed Hazel Drew and she kept quiet about it, to protect herself and her family. As soon as the matter of the inquest was settled, Minnie quit her position with the Harrisons and went to stay with family. When she returned to Troy, she was married to a man connected to the local Republican Party who soon began making a good living for himself in the spring water business. Certainly, Minnie had plenty of opportunities to get married before, but had no interest. Perhaps if she did have blackmail on the local partisans—or if Hazel did—Minnie put it to work. This turns D.A. O'Brien's "sweats" of Aunt Minnie into theater.

We know Julia Drew was a superstitious person. She wouldn't want her dead daughter laying in repose across the street from her killer. We know from the news reports that on at least one occasion when the pressmen turned up at the Cary home, John Drew was there on site. The dutiful father clearly had some interest in the Carys even after Hazel's property was fully removed from their home.

This explains, in my mind, why Hazel's family moved her grave on the day of the service. Keeping the family safe meant keeping a low profile. However, burying Hazel next to her killer's house was too much to ask. This change would have been expensive but Hazel's body was still in Sand Lake at the Larkin Brother's Funeral Home and Hazel's parents had collected her insurance policy, which would provide the funds to bury their daughter as they chose. Hazel Drew was the first of her family to be buried at Brookside, but eventually most of her immediate family, including her parents, would join her.

I believe the moving grave is a powerful "tell" that Hazel's family had some inkling of her killer. If the family merely wanted a more convenient place to bury her, there were cemeteries in Sand Lake that were closer to the funeral parlor. Hazel's family wanted her both away from her murderer and somewhere familiar, that she could call home forever.

WAS IT A COVER-UP?

Obviously, I am convinced that Professor Cary was Hazel Drew's killer. I am further convinced that District Attorney Jarvis P. O'Brien worked to cover up that fact. We know that Cary and O'Brien had mutual business interests, working for railroad development in Troy and its surrounds. We know they were both prominent Republicans, serving at various times in government together. By 1910 they were both living in the same neighborhood. The two men moved in the same circles and shared the same agenda. They knew each other and they certainly must have been allies, sharing the same commercial and civic goals.

O'Brien must have known from the get-go that his murderer was someone within his own class. He was no fool. He also had to know, even with a primitive knowledge of criminology, that a prime suspect was Hazel's boss. No doubt after leaving Taborton Road following his first visit, O'Brien drove the six miles to Whitman Court, pulled into the Cary's driveway, looked at the Professor's tires, and had his man.

The case was in the sheriff's jurisdiction, but O'Brien kept a handle on it. The New York police took an interest, but O'Brien kept a lid on it. He publicly sweated Minnie Taylor in the press, while soft balling her on the stand at the inquest to the point that the pressman demanded that Coroner Strope let *them* ask questions.

At various times O'Brien appeared to move toward arresting Frank Smith or Will Taylor, only to blow them off as simpletons. He made hay out of Magner only to buy his alibi when it was clearly ironclad. O'Brien let Will Clemens run rabid in the press, allowing the man to publish the "C.E.S." letter and the goofy Knight of the Napp Kin letter without offering a single confirmation of their authenticity. O'Brien entertained a theory from a demented man from Vermont. He spoke of Trojans finding clues in their dreams.

The only time Jarvis O'Brien ever sought to correct the truly out of line public record regarding the investigation into Hazel Drew's death was when Mrs. Drew provided her theory that a prominent man in the town who had hypnotic power was her likely killer. As we see from Professor Cary's attestation in Sage's hypnotism booklet, he was the only suspect who fit that description and O'Brien needed to shut it down.

There is at least one other character in this tale who had

direct business ties to Professor Cary: Dr. Edward Knauff. Knauff was Hazel Drew's dentist and his son, William, was about Hazel's age and was one of Professor Cary's engineering students. By 1910, Dr. Knauff was serving as a Director of the Pioneer Building-Loan Savings Association Bank, with *Professor Cary* serving as an Auditor. Did this little bank provide D.A. O'Brien the loan to build his nice home off Pawling Avenue near Professor Cary? Did it fund any of the various railroad projects ongoing? Did it make the loan to Mr. Filieu that allowed him to start his prosperous water business? We do not know.

We do know that Cary business partner and Dentist Dr. Knauff weighed into the Drew case in such a way as to support Peter Cipperly's story of seeing Hazel on the Albia car with a young man. This also might further explain his son William Knauff's odd behavior in quitting school and getting out of Troy. If William Knauff really were a close friend of Hazel Drew's – intimate or otherwise – he, like Hazel's family, no doubt suspected Cary of the crime. Knowing that Cary was an associate of his father's would drive a wedge between the two men. As with Minnie Taylor leaving town and Frank Jones remaining out of town, after Hazel died it probably felt easier for William Knauff to simply give up his field of study and make a life elsewhere. Which he did.

On July 21 the *Albany Times Union*— and virtually no other paper in the region—reported the story of Jarvis O'Brien meeting in secret for over an hour with a man in his office, whom he assisted in departing the courthouse without being seen or subjected to reporters' interviews. The *Times Union* reporter got a look at the fellow as he snuck out and reported that he was slender and had a "sandy mustache." He also reported that this man was unfamiliar to everyone involved in the case. As we know, Professor Cary himself had a moustache and was never a public suspect. If Professor Cary were wearing his hat, his balding head would have gone unnoticed, thus no one would have tied him to the mystery man with the "receding" forehead.

The 21st was a pivotal day in the investigation. In addition to revelations related to the Hoffay's supposed witnessing of a runabout at the pond, this is also the day John Magner was fully implicated. The case would conclude in only ten more days. In the chaos this would have been a prime opportunity to have a quick liaise with Professor Cary. I don't love the quality of this clue, but it's worth considering.

O'Brien wasn't rewarded for his efforts in covering up Hazel's killer. He lost his office and was never elected again. After 1908 both he and Cary were out of politics for good. The City Engineer's job meant so little to Cary that he walked on its big salary in favor of other opportunities. The ties between these men weren't political – in their case I believe their politics was a means to a bigger end. In 1908 only one force was greater than the Two Parties and that was the American Empire Builders, the railroads.

O'Brien and Cary were linked through their railroad projects. Cary and Knauff were linked through their banking work, which no doubt had ties to the railroads, or at least to the building and construction projects that arose because of railroad expansion. There is one other interesting connection we need to consider.

From day one Jarvis O'Brien tried to chalk Hazel Drew's death up to suicide. He continually stated if it weren't for the medical men, he'd mark her death down as a suicide. Not satisfied with the opinions of the doctors who performed her autopsy, he called in his own man, Dr. Clinton Bradford Herrick, the famous railroad surgeon to argue for the suicide theory, as outlined above. This was O'Brien's Hail Mary pass to get the thing ruled as something other than murder.

Dr. Harrick and O'Brien were in fact cronies. In 1899 when Dr. Herrick's book was published, he was a physician for the Fitchburg Railroad. This is the line that connected Troy and the rest of eastern New York State with Vermont and Massachusetts and was merged with the Boston and Maine Railroad in 1900. O'Brien was working for the Boston and Maine in 1900, so it stands to reason both he and Dr. Herrick had worked for the Fitchburg, the rail line passing through their town, before it merged with the B&M. By 1900 both men are being paid by the same outfit. Both O'Brien and Cary are working on projects to push Troy north and east, around the Taconic Mountains, to link it with mighty Boston.

If Professor Cary were taken down on a murder charge a lot of projects could go down with him, not to mention the embarrassment felt by the city of Troy and RPI. The massive project to build a second track along the B&M's entire New York spur as the result of the 1906 accident in Lansingburgh would be in jeopardy. By 1908 Cary was no longer Troy City Engineer, but he clearly was into enough additional work that he did not feel the loss of the revenue. No doubt this was railroad money.

Other writers have speculated that Hazel had spent her entire life in the home of wealthy, well-connected men. The same was true of Minnie Taylor. Between the two of them they no doubt had enough secrets in their heads to bring down all of Troy, half of Albany, and a handful of men in Washington. Is there any evidence that Hazel had access to actionable blackmail?

Well, yes, because it seems like Minnie Taylor used it. She clammed up and got herself away from Whitman Court and Pawling Avenue, only to return to town wired to a smalltime GOP man who very soon was making a nice living for himself. Without ever working another day in her life, Minnie was able to eventually afford a home, some automobiles, and provide a legacy for her family and church, well after her husband's death.

Perhaps Hazel and the Professor got up to a little no good the last weekend of her life and Cary wanted it to go a little further. Hazel, not exactly being the type who loved men rejected him. Something happened and she was either fired or left his employment. One or the other parties sought a reconciliation so Hazel picked a secret, safe spot she knew well in close proximity to both her uncle and brother. The Professor could get there but it would have to be late. The meeting was set.

When they met, it was around midnight, she had already heard his car coming up Taborton Road. Seeing her flash of white shirtwaist— the one she wore on their weekend away—he pulled his car down to the water. Maybe he could talk her out of whatever she was planning and drive her home. They had a chat. She wasn't interested in going home. She was ready to get out of Troy and finally get to New York City. She'd gone there just the day before and she was certain it was time. She had friends she could stay with to get started. Is all she needed was a little seed money. After all she was down to her last nickel.

Cary argued he'd paid her final wages, all that she was owed. But Hazel insisted their arrangement was different now. He wasn't buying her labor, but her silence. For a small price, she'd walk away, spend the night with her uncle, make her way back to Troy Union Station, where her suitcase was stowed, and hop the next train to the Metropolis. He'd never see her again.

Maybe he said something stupid like, "well I want to see you again" and she tossed her head back and laughed. Not the type of man to be mocked, the Professor got enraged and shoved the girl. Caught off guard by a man she trusted and knew to be non-violent, she fell back, was constrained by her clothes, and hit her head on that awful rock. Her glasses fell off just as the contusion caused by her fall stopped her heart.

From there we know the scenario. Professor Cary, unable to be caught out like that, covered his tracks by tossing Hazel's body into the pond and fled. Why not? She had threatened *him*. And not just him but everything he stood for and everything he was working on.

When Jarvis O'Brien came knocking on his door a few days later, he knew he was safe. The two men concocted a scheme to try to get the thing marked down as suicide. Cary's job was to lay low, work on the Nicholson matter, not talk to the press, and get ready for those August railroad surveying classes. Hazel was just a domestic – people wouldn't care. If they did care, O'Brien could handle it. If things got too hot, they'd try to find some dupe to pin it on.

With the handing down of Coroner Strope's verdict the investigation into Hazel Drew's death was forgotten almost immediately. The publication of Will Clemon's stories in the

Pulitzer press created the narrative every investigator has followed up to the writing of this book.

Hazel's trunk wasn't packed with love letters, but with missives from childhood friends and notes from doctors. She didn't travel around the east coast whoring it up. She never had an abortion, she had the flu. She wasn't living an unseemly double-life but having fun with guy pals who liked to pick up the tab. She was not bashed over the head as the work of an assassin but slipped and fell from a push. Hazel was, it turns out, a good girl who fell into a bad situation and found herself taken advantage of by the man who hired her and whom she trusted. Maybe she should have walked away from Whitman Court forever, gotten on the *Saratoga*, and just never looked back. But in the end, tasting a bit of the good life had probably made the temptation too strong and she decided to try to play the same game as the power brokers she'd worked for her entire life. If that's the case, I don't think we have a right to blame her.

Though it was an act of rage and an accident, Professor Cary killed Hazel Drew.

[1] The United Nations "Global Study on Homicide," (2019) is the most recent source to comprehensively outline global homicide statistics.

[2] Anita D. Tirots and Michael R. Rand in the paper "Violent Crime by Strangers and Non-Strangers," published in the *Bureau of Justice Statistics Special Report* in 1987 provide an early and comprehensive understanding of crime statistics in the United States before crime rates began to precipitously drop.

[3] *Evening Star*, July 24, 1908.

[4] *Troy Record*, July 18, 1908.

[5] Professor Cary's name was *often* misspelled in contemporary publications with the "E." However, I have confirmed he was the only E.R. Cary/Carey to serve on the RPI faculty during his tenure.

THIS ISN'T OVER

CHAPTER 23

Whenever I visit Troy and the surrounds I am perpetually on the lookout for photos and postcards from 1908 that might contain a clue to Hazel Drew's murder. In the weeks following the discovery of her body *thousands* of people visited Teal's Pond, and hundreds of people snapped pictures of the pond and the undertaker's office. Somewhere in grandma's attic or in some Watervliet junk store are photos taken of the scene of her death. There are letters written by Hazel to her friends sandwiched into an album with pressed flowers. If Mark Frost's grandmother knew the story of Hazel Drew, then so did others. They wrote what they knew down, they told others. There are clues still out there and with awareness from books like this, people in Troy and Sand Lake's old Victorian homes will know to look out for them.

More resources will eventually become available online that could give us an understanding of Professor Cary's whereabouts and business dealings. More train records. More hotel records. More public documents.

There will also be more red herrings. For instance, the Ithaca *Chronicle* of August 13, 1908, reported dramatically that Jarvis O'Brien had under suspicion a prominent young man of Troy who had written numerous love letters to Hazel. At any minute, the paper reported, an arrest would be made! Nothing came of it.

Though this book is finished, this investigation will never be over. It is my sincere hope that telling this story *now*, as I have told it, will help to open new areas of investigation. I think people in Hazel's day knew who did it. I think people had suspicions.

I believe I have solved Hazel Drew's murder and that the case I've laid out in this book is the most logical and credible explanation for what happened based on the evidence. There are more clues to find and more story to tell, even if it's not by me. This isn't over. Thanks to *Twin Peaks,* Hazel Drew's memory will live on. If I've done anything with this book, it is to bring into focus Hazel's real life and character, in striking contrast with a sexist and sensationalized tabloid representation. In so doing, this frees us from the simplistic and insulting binary of *good girl* versus *bad girl,* which only serves to dehumanize a woman operating with her own agency. This is the tragic story of a person whose life was cut short suddenly, cruelly, and with the full complicity of the men of power who covered for the killer. The evidence presented here is damning. I hope this story inspires you to keep digging for the truth, because it is not over. Hazel Drew will have the last word.

The author's Hazel Drew "crazy wall" in his former study,
where his Covid-fueled obsession with Hazel's murder
developed. Photo by the author.

THE END
Or is it?

Bibliography

SOURCES

The primary source material for the preceding manuscript are newspaper accounts from June, July, and August 1908. In addition, a number of books and other references were consulted. Below is a select bibliography of key sources.

NEWSPAPERS

Alexandria Gazette and Virginia Advertiser
Albany Times Union
Barre Daily Times
Bennington Evening Banner
Cameron County Press
Citizen Republican
Detroit Times
Deutscher Correspondent
Evening Journal
Evening Star
Evening Statesman
Evening Tribune
Evening World
Fargo Forum and Daily Republican
Farmers Leader
Greene County Herald
Hattiesburg News
Honesdale Citizen
Kingsbury County Independent
Lewiston Evening Teller
Marion Daily Mirror
Morning Journal Courier
New York Daily Tribune
New York Times
New York World
Ocala Evening Star
Omaha Bee
Perth Amboy Evening News
Richmond Palladium and Sun Telegram
Special to the Argus

Spirit of the Age
Star
Thrice-A-Week World
Times Dispatch
Topeka Daily Star Journal
Troy Daily Record
Troy Evening Record
Troy Northern Budget
Troy Press
Troy Times
Valentine Democrat
Washington Herald
Washington Post
Washington Times
Waterbury Evening Democrat

SELECTED BOOKS

Bushman, David and Givens, Mark T. *Murder at Teal's Pond: Hazel Drew and the Murder that Inspired Twin Peaks.* Seattle, Thomas and Mercer, 2022.

Clay, Alice. *The Agony Column of the "Times."* London, Chatto and Windus, 1881.

Herrick, Clinton B. *Railway Surgery: A Handbook on the Management of Injuries.* New York, William Wood and Company, 1899.

Hughes, Ron. *Who Killed Hazel Drew?: Unraveling the Clues to the Tragic Murder of a Pretty Servant Girl.* Pennsauken, NJ, BookBaby, 2017.

Troy, City Corporation of. *Two Centuries of Public Service: History of the Troy Water Works.* Troy, N.Y., City of Troy, 1977.

Turbin, Carole. *Working Women of Collar City: Gender, Class, and Community in Troy, New York, 1864-86.* Champaign, University of Illinois Press, 1992.

Acknowledgments

I am heavily indebted to several people for their assistance and support in researching and writing this book. First and foremost, to my wife Vickie for her extreme patience in allowing me the freedom to pursue this research, which included trips to Troy, New York City, Burlington, Vermont, and points in between, often at a moment's notice, as well as being a co-detective and research partner throughout the investigation. Many of the sources were located by Vickie who is an academic librarian and one of the best researchers in the business. To Vickie, I apologize for all of the stress and strife this project caused, but I couldn't have told this story without you.

Secondly, I want to thank Leza Cantoral, my friend of many years and the publisher of this book. It was Leza and her husband Christoph Paul's move to Troy that allowed us all to discover Hazel Drew. Leza acted as the spiritual inspiration for this book and was not only a great host during research trips, but a constant partner on the road. All of that thanks is in addition to the professional tasks related to the publication of the manuscript. Leza has been, more than anyone else, Hazel's living voice throughout this investigation.

I thank Elena Miloh Gorgevska for invaluable editorial assistance and for acting as a constant sounding board. Miloh also served as a research partner during my New York City investigations, which proved to be tremendously rewarding. I hope that we will be able to work together on similar projects in the future.

The staff of various institutions also deserve thanks, especially the Troy Public Library, the Albany Public Library, the New York State Library, the Sand Lake Town Library, and the Schenectady Public Library. I also have to thank the very patient staff of my "hangouts" during this project, especially Ted's Fish Fry in Watervliet, Manory's Restaurant in Troy, the Town Tavern in Averill Park, the Old Northender Pub in Burlington, and the El Dorado Bar in Troy. These are all excellent, historic establishments deserving of your patronage. Finally, I must thank Lisa Marie Basile for being present the night I found the "key" that opened the door to this case.

ABOUT THE AUTHOR

Dr. Jerry C. Drake is a career civil servant, former professor of history, all-around amateur detective, with a wide-ranging educational background to include degrees in anthropology and United States history. This is his first foray into true crime. His short stories have appeared in two CLASH anthologies: *Tragedy Queens: Stories Inspired by Lana Del Rey & Sylvia Plath* and *Walk Hand In Hand Into Extinction: Stories Inspired by True Detective.*

Also by CLASH Books

THE MAN WHO SAW SECONDS

Alexander Boldizar

TRAGEDY QUEENS: STORIES INSAPIRED BY LANA DEL REY
& SYLVIA PLATH

Edited by Leza Cantoral

THE PINK AGAVE MOTEL

V. Castro

CHARCOAL

Garrett Cook

LETTERS TO THE PURPLE SATIN KILLER

Joshua Chaplinsky

I DIED TOO, BUT THEY HAVEN'T BURIED ME YET

Ross Jeffery

CATHERINE THE GHOST

Kathe Koja

EVERYTHING THE DARKNESS EATS

Eric LaRocca

HELENA

Claire Smith

THE BLACK TREE ATOP THE HILL

Karla Yvette

www.ingramcontent.com/pod-product-compliance
Lightning Source LLC
Chambersburg PA
CBHW021716120626
46545CB00004B/1594